AF251042

ALABAMA IMPACT

Contemporary Artists with Alabama Ties

Mobile Museum of Art ▼ Huntsville Museum of Art

Mobile Museum of Art
ACKNOWLEDGEMENTS

Almost five years ago, the idea for this exhibition was born. With the addition of new staff at our museum in Mobile and the Huntsville Museum of Art, it has grown and developed into this major exhibition. This exhibition was organized for two very specific purposes. All too often, Alabama is thought of as a sleepy, backward state from which no worthy effort could ever come or flourish. We wanted to make certain that this show dispells that myth for the visual arts. Similarly, we aimed to foster in the citizens of Alabama more pride in the artists who claim that "Alabama has had an impact" on their lives and works.

This exhibition presents a very good crosssection of current work by a select group of artists but is by no means all-inclusive. Some artists we wanted to include could not be contacted or did not respond, others could not participate because of prior commitments, and we were forced, based on our budget and space limitations, to pass over others. We also did not get into the other rich arenas of Alabama's visual arts, particularly crafts and folk, outsider, or visionary art. This leaves us opportunities for another day and another show. You also will note that we tried to borrow works directly from artists whenever possible. We, however, do wish to thank the museums, galleries, and private collectors who loaned us work when we ran into difficulties. In particular: William H. Bengtson, Phyllis Kind Gallery, Chicago; Michael Bliss, Max Protech Gallery, New York; Martha Connell, Connell Gallery, Atlanta; Stuart Horodner, Horodner Romley Gallery, New York; Aaron Miller, Louis K. Meisel Gallery, New York; Arthur Roger, Arthur Roger Gallery, New Orleans; Joseph D. Rowand, Somerhill Gallery, Chapel Hill; Monty Stabler, Monty Stabler Galleries, Birmingham; and Mark Del Vecchio, Garth Clark Gallery, New York must be singled out for their generous assistance.

A very special acknowledgement goes out to our outstanding curator, Dr. Paul W. Richelson. The lion's share of the work on this exhibition was done by him. He has spent countless days visiting and corresponding with artists, preparing contracts, pouring over slides, photographs and vitas, compiling catalogue data, and traveling around the country to bring these artworks together. I salute him for the terrific job he has done and also acknowledge his assistants, Rowena Van Hoof, registrar, and Donan Klooz, preparator. I also would like to express appreciation to Peter J. Baldaia, chief curator and interim director at the Huntsville Museum of Art who came into this project last year and has been a great help. The Huntsville staff has been very supportive of the project and we thank them for their efforts. I owe a special debt of gratitude to David Robb, Jr., who served as director of the Huntsville Museum of Art during the formative stages of this exhibition. David took a keen interest in the project and was willing to join forces with us in making this a major statewide effort. Without his help and the support of our grant application to the Alabama State Council on the Arts, we would not have secured the funding for this catalogue. A very special thanks also goes to the staff, panel, and council members of the Alabama State Council on the Arts who awarded us an expanded assistance grant which supported the amplification of the project.

In conclusion, we dedicate this catalogue to those artists who have been influenced by their time in Alabama. They have and will continue to enrich the artistic life of this state and the nation. We also hope this exhibition and document will aid current and future generations of artists who consider the "Alabama Impact" of those presented in this show at the Mobile Museum of Art and the Huntsville Museum of Art in 1995.

Joseph B. Schenk, Director
Mobile Museum of Art, Mobile, Alabama

Huntsville Museum of Art
ACKNOWLEDGEMENTS

The Huntsville Museum of Art is very pleased to present *Alabama Impact: Contemporary Artists with Alabama Ties* in collaboration with the Mobile Museum of Art. This landmark exhibition represents an ambitious joint endeavor between two major Alabama museums, extending and underscoring each institution's commitment to regional contemporary art. A project of this nature and scale is no easy undertaking. The Mobile Museum of Art deserves high praise for its essential role in organizing the exhibition. My thanks to Joseph B. Schenk, director of the Mobile Museum of Art, for his relaxed and professional assistance with project budgeting and tracking. Special thanks go to curator Paul W. Richelson, for his informed selection of artists and works, detailed assembly of biographical data, and insightful introduction to the exhibition catalogue.

I commend the staff of the Huntsville Museum of Art for its commitment, energy, and support through several phases of this project. Thanks to former director David Robb, Jr. for conceptualizing the exhibition with Joseph Schenk and providing a smooth transition for my subsequent management of our phase of project responsibilities. Several staff members deserve particular praise for their essential contributions: education director Deborah Taylor for formulating programs to complement the exhibition; registrar David Reyes for coordinating transportation for the Huntsville venue of the exhibition; exhibition designer Joe Washington and preparator Stuart Siniard for their installation magic; publicist Marylyn Coffey for exhibition promotion; and development director Leigh Tucker for fundraising efforts. I additionally thank Huntsville graphic designer Bettye Altherr Howard for a handsomely designed exhibition announcement and catalogue and for her conscientious effort in coordinating and supervising all aspects of catalogue production.

I am grateful to the Alabama State Council on the Arts for supporting this project through major funding which enabled the Huntsville Museum of Art to co-publish this fine exhibition catalogue. The Museum deeply appreciates the Council's commitment to enhancing the quality of life in Alabama through support of visual arts projects such as this.

Finally, I extend my appreciation to all the artists represented in the exhibition for providing dazzling proof of Alabama's remarkable impact on the regional, national, and international art scene.

Peter J. Baldaia, Chief Curator and Interim Director
Huntsville Museum of Art, Huntsville, Alabama

INTRODUCTION

While several recent museum exhibitions, most notably *Southern Expressions* (1988-1991), a series of projects at the High Museum, Atlanta, Georgia; and *Looking South: A Different Dixie* (1988), an exhibition at the Birmingham Museum of Art, Birmingham, Alabama, have widened awareness of the contemporary visual arts scene in the new South, ***Alabama Impact: Contemporary Artists with Alabama Ties,*** focuses on artists associated with one state. While many states proudly lay claim to artists whose fame was established elsewhere, many artists are probably never associated with any special political/geographical place while that connection might provide insight. Simply said, this exhibition was conceived as a bringing together of contemporary artists who have gained recognition in wider contemporary American and international arenas and who have a special connection with the State of Alabama. This cooperative project, made possible, in part, by the generous assistance of the Alabama State Council on the Arts, seeks to recognize and document those artists with a special Alabama connection. Curatorially this has not led to a rigid definition of what this Alabama connection might be. Quite naturally, artists who were born here are included, assuming that if they did not stay long, family ties maintained a continuous bond. Visual artists born elsewhere but who lived in or currently make Alabama their home were invited. These are the most obvious associations to be made with any state. No less significant are those individuals who came to Alabama for their education. Logically included are the artist/teachers, some who were briefly in the state and others who spent most of their professional lives here, participating in an educational process in which they influenced both students and communities alike over the last 40 years, as a contemporary art scene emerged in Alabama.

What can be said of the assembled works of these sixty-seven artists in the exhibition? As there was no attempt at thematic or stylistic selection, the results are, not surprisingly, parallel with the contemporary scene today anywhere: something for everyone. Abstraction and figuration exist side by side. Some observations are possible, but no conclusions. Clearly, for the vast majority of artists who left Alabama to establish careers elsewhere, the preferred city was New York. This pattern continues today, with younger artists Richmond Burton and Matt Nolen well established there. More individuals than before have managed to continue to reside in Alabama while becoming known elsewhere, and most have educational institutions as their primary source of income. One might ask whether, with all the artists selected because of their association with a particular place, there is a strong vision of regional identity, of roots (as is so often posited for Southern art). Well, yes, but not as much as you might expect and not always in an obvious way. Alabama is blessed with great physical diversity, from mountains, flat lands, river byways, and the waters of the Gulf of Mexico, much of it bearing the evidence of change through farming, fishing, industry, lumbering, and tourism. There is also wild and unspoiled nature. To be in Alabama is to be aware of all this. It certainly is not vast physical beauty in the grand tradition of American landscape painting which is visible in the exhibition. More often, there is a vernacular sense of a locality occupied, perhaps abandoned, maybe brutalized, especially when it is identified as Alabama landscape, as in the photographs of William Christenberry. The artists hold few romantic illusions, rather a fascination with the banal aspects of place and geography, nothing unique to Alabama artists. There is an attachment to depicting interior spaces, an odd outgrowth, perhaps, of an interest in locale, home, and hearth. This sense of place also is recalled historically and culturally. The artists and their art reveal unresolved racial questions, remembered and ongoing. These artists are not disconnected from the issues of their times: AIDS, debatable social icons, cultural clichés, the environment, and disquieting interpersonal conflicts of the late 20th century all find expression.

A few miscellaneous observations need to be made. The mix of artists in the exhibition substantiates the importance of women artists to the Alabama contemporary scene, much as elsewhere in the United States. This is nothing new for Alabama, although in the last century women like Ann Goldthwaite and Louise Lyons Heustis had to leave the state for training and careers. Ceramics, glass, photography, and sculpture are mediums which serve the expressive purposes of these Alabama-connected artists to no less a degree than for creative individuals in other parts of the country today.

What these artists share is an Alabama experience which, in subtle and varied ways, influenced each life and thereby the ideas and creative visual statements of each individual. No orthodoxy of expression prevails, but the ties are there and the artists have confirmed them by their gracious willingness to participate in this project.

Paul W. Richelson, Curator of American Art
Mobile Museum of Art

The Exhibition

Fathers and Sons, 1994, oil on linen

Jere H. Allen

lives in Oxford, Mississippi
born 1944 in Selma, Alabama
1970 BFA Ringling School of Art, Sarasota, Florida
1972 MFA University of Tennessee, Knoxville

selected recent exhibitions

1994 *Solo Exhibition,* Gulfcoast Community College, Gautier, Mississippi
    Solo Exhibition, Carol Robinson Gallery, New Orleans (also 1993, 1992, 1990)
1993 *Solo Exhibition,* Memphis College of Art, Memphis, Tennessee
    Solo Exhibition, Jones County Community College, Ellisville, Mississippi
    Figurative Art: The Human Experience, Partnership Gallery, Montgomery, Alabama
    Group Exhibition, Isabel Comer Anderson Museum, Sylacauga, Alabama
    Bi-State Faculty Exhibition, Meridian Museum of Art, Meridian, Mississippi
1992 *Solo Exhibition,* Finley Gallery, Birmingham, Alabama
    Solo Exhibition, Whiting Art Center, Fairhope, Alabama
    Solo Exhibition, Automatic Slims, Memphis, Tennessee
    Solo Exhibition, Brenau College, Gainsville, Georgia
    Annual Bi-State Art Competition, Meridian Museum of Art, Meridian, Mississippi,
      (also 1989)
    Gala '92, National Invitational Exhibition, Brenau College, Gainsville, Georgia
      (also 1989)
    Spotlight on Southeast Artists-XI, Trinity School, Atlanta, Georgia
1991 *Rest, Sleep, and Dream Show,* Altman-Riddick Museum, Coleman Center,
     York, Alabama
    Group Exhibition, Carol Robinson Gallery, New Orleans, Louisiana
1990 *Solo Exhibition,* Delta State University, Cleveland, Mississippi
    Solo Exhibition, Collector's Gallery, Nashville, Tennessee
    Ten, The 1990 Mid-Year Exhibition, Part One, Memphis Center for Contemporary
     Art, Memphis, Tennessee
    Five Artists, New Center for Creative Awareness, Sarasota, Florida
1989 *Jere Allen Bilder aus America 1971 bis 1989 "Ironie und tiefere Bedeutung,"* Der
     Kunstkreis Hameln, Hameln, West Germany (traveled to Oldenburger
     Kunstverein; Städtische Galerie, Paderborn, West Germany)
    Group Exhibition, Carol Robinson Gallery, New Orleans, Louisiana
    Group Exhibition, Collector's Gallery, Nashville, Tennessee
    Birmingham Biennial V, Birmingham Art Association, Birmingham, Alabama
    National Invitational Drawing Exhibition, Emporia State University, Emporia,
     Kansas (traveled)

selected honors, awards, grants

1992 *Visual Arts Award,* Mississippi Institute of Arts and Letters, Jackson, Mississippi
1989 *Award, "Annual Bi-State Art Competition,"* Meridian Museum of Art,
     Meridian, Mississippi
1979 *Fulbright-Hays Group Fellowship Grant,* Costa Rica, Central America
1975 *Bellaman Foundation Grant,* Jackson, Mississippi
1966 *Selby Foundation Grant,* Sarasota, Florida

Taliesen Valley, 1991, cibachrome print laminated to plexiglas

Paula Barr

lives in New York, New York
born 1945 in Philadelphia, Pennsylvania;
   resided Mobile, Alabama 1961-1963
1967 BFA Boston University, Boston, Massachusetts
Taught Mobile College (Mobile University) and Spring
   Hill College, Mobile, Alabama, 1977-1978

selected recent exhibitions

1994-1992
Commissions-In-Progress
   Mobile Infirmary Medical Center, 12' x 72', Atrium interior wall, panoramic glass photo/tile
      mural, Mobile, Alabama
   Bellview Hospital, two 4' x 7' windows of glass photo/tiles, renovated entrance, and two
      3 1/2' x 10' panoramic murals, Staff Cafeteria, Health & Hospitals Corp.,
      New York, New York
   VA Hospital, three 5' x 15' panoramic photo banners in atrium, Veterans Administration
      Hospital, New York, New York
   MTA Arts-for-Transit, Subway 2' x 200' panoramic photo/tile installation, interior and
      exterior walls, platform mezzanine, SOHO Station, New York, New York
   PANY & NJ George Washington Bridge Administration Building, 2' x 22' photo/tile 360°
      degree panorama of bridge and shoreline, exterior to interior photo/tile architectural band,
      New York, New York
   George Washington Bridge Communications Center, 2 site-specific photo murals for the Port
      Authority of New York and New Jersey
1991 *Operation Welcome Home, NYC,* panoramic portfolio for AGFA Films, USA

selected honors, awards, grants

1989 *Bronze Medal,* New Jersey Art Directors
1988 *Imagination Award,* Champion Paper (also 1987)
1976 *Artist in Residence,* Z.B.S. Foundation
1974 *Fellowship Recipient,* National Endowment for the Arts, Washington, D.C.

Spirit House—Lotus, 1991, mixed media on wood

Raine Bedsole

lives in New Orleans, Louisiana
born 1960 in Mobile, Alabama
1983 BFA Auburn University,
   Auburn, Alabama
1989 MFA San Francisco Art
   Institute, San Francisco, California

selected recent exhibitions

1994 *Solo Exhibition,* Marguerite Oestreicher Fine Art, New Orleans, Louisiana
   Summer Group Show, Stephen Haller Gallery, New York, New York
   Underexposed, Contemporary Arts Center, New Orleans, Louisiana
1993 *Timely and Timeless,* The Aldrich Museum of Contemporary Art, Ridgefield,
   Connecticut
1992 *Solo Exhibition,* Cumberland Gallery, Nashville, Tennessee
   Compact Competition, Louisiana State University, Baton Rouge, Louisiana
   New American Talent: Eighth Exhibition, Laguna Gloria Art Museum,
   Austin, Texas
   Selections, University of New Orleans, New Orleans, Louisiana
1991 *Solo Exhibition,* Suzanne Dey Gallery, Menlo Park, California
   Tom Peyton Memorial Exhibition, Alexandria Museum of Art, Alexandria,
   Louisiana
1990 *Solo Exhibition,* Hall-Barnett Gallery, New Orleans, Louisiana
1989 *LA5,* Kentuck Art Center, Northport, Alabama
   SFAI-MFA Exhibition, Pier 3, San Francisco, California

selected honors, awards, grants

1992 *Juror's Merit Award, "Compact Competition,"* Louisiana State University,
   Baton Rouge, Louisiana

Roger Brown

lives in Chicago, Illinois
born 1941 in Hamilton, Alabama;
  resided Opelika, Alabama 1945-1960
1960 David Lipscomb College, Nashville, Tennessee
1961 University of Tennessee, Nashville, Tennessee
1962-1964 American Academy of Art, Chicago, Illinois
1968 BFA The School of the Art Institute of Chicago,
  Chicago, Illinois
1970 MFA The School of the Art Institute of Chicago,
  Chicago, Illinois

selected recent exhibitions

1994 *Solo Exhibition,* Phyllis Kind Gallery, Chicago, Illinois
Elvis + Marilyn, 2 x Immortal, Institute of Contemporary Art, Boston,
  Massachusetts (traveled)
Thirty Something: A 30th Anniversary Celebration, Fine Arts Museum of
  the South, Mobile, Alabama
1993 *Chicago Art Invitational,* Union League Club, Chicago, Illinois
Imagery: Incongruous Juxtapositions, Phyllis Kind Gallery, Chicago, Illinois
1992 *Solo Exhibition,* Phyllis Kind Gallery, New York, New York
Parallel Visions: Modern Artists and Outsider Art, Los Angeles County Museum
  of Art, Los Angeles, California (traveled to Kunsthalle, Basel, Switzerland; Centro
  de Arte Reina Sofía, Madrid, Spain; and Setagaya Art Museum, Tokyo, Japan)
Mind and Beast: Contemporary Artists and the Animal Kingdom, Leigh Yawkey
  Woodson Art Museum, Wausau, Wisconsin (traveled to The Art Museum of South
  Texas, Corpus Christi, Texas; Tuscon Museum of Art, Tuscon, Arizona; The
  Canton Art Institute, Canton, Ohio; and Fort Wayne Museum of Art, Fort Wayne,
  Indiana)
Face to Face: Self-Portraits by Chicago Artists, The Chicago Cultural Center,
  Chicago, Illinois
My Father's House Has Many Mansions, Phyllis Kind Gallery, New York, New York
From America's Studio: Twelve Contemporary Masters, The Art Institute of
  Chicago, Chicago, Illinois
1991 *Solo Exhibition,* Phyllis Kind Gallery, Chicago, Illinois
The Realm of the Coin, Emily Lowe Gallery, Hofstra University, Hempstead,
  New York (traveled)
Revelations: Artists Look at Religions, The School of the Art Institute of Chicago,
  Gallery 2, Chicago, Illinois
The Art of Advocacy, The Aldrich Museum of Contemporary Art, Ridgefield,
  Connecticut
Vital Signs: Art in and About Atlanta, The New Nexus Gallery, Nexus
  Contemporary Art Center, Atlanta, Georgia
*Image and Likeness: Figurative Works from the Permanent Collection of the
  Whitney Museum of American Art,* Whitney Museum of American Art,
  New York, New York
1990 *Solo Exhibition,* Arthur Roger Gallery, New Orleans, Louisiana
Solo Exhibition, David Heath Gallery, Atlanta, Georgia
Word As Image/American Art 1960-1990, Milwaukee Art Museum, Milwaukee,
  Wisconsin (traveled to Oklahoma City Art Museum, Oklahoma City, Oklahoma
  and Contemporary Arts Museum, Houston, Texas)
Portraits of a Kind, Phyllis Kind Gallery, Chicago, Illinois
Speaking Out: Five Centuries of Social Commentary in Printmaking, Telfair
  Academy of Arts and Sciences, Savannah, Georgia

Americana/Benton, O'Keefe, Rivera & Hartley, 1988, oil on canvas

Of His Bones are Coral Made, 1993, oil on linen

Richmond Burton

lives in New York, New York
born 1960 in Talladega, Alabama
1982 BA Rice University, Houston, Texas
1984 Bachelor of Architecture Rice
   University, Houston, Texas

selected recent exhibitions

1994 *Solo Exhibition,* Matthew Marks Gallery, New York, New York (also 1991)
   New York Abstract Painting, Salvatore Ala Gallery, New York, New York
   The Inward Eye, Laura Carpenter Fine Art, Santa Fe, New Mexico
1993 *Solo Exhibition,* Rhona Hoffman Gallery, Chicago, Illinois
   Solo Exhibition, Turner and Byrne Gallery, Dallas, Texas
   I am the Enunciator, curated by Christian Leigh, Thread Waxing Space,
      New York, New York
   Daylight Savings, curated by Jonathan Hammer, John Berggruen Gallery,
      San Francisco, California
   Gentleman Friends, University Art Museum, University of California at
      Berkeley, Berkeley, California
   Jours Tranquilles a Clichy, curated by Alain Kirili, Paris, France
   Four Centuries of Drawing 1593-1993, Kohn Abrams Gallery,
      Los Angeles, California
   The Return of the Exquisite Corpse, The Drawing Center, New York, New York
   *30th Anniversary Exhibition to Benefit the Foundation for Contemporary
      Performance Arts,* Leo Castelli Gallery, New York, New York
1992 *Richmond Burton Bilder, Arbeiten auf Papier und Skizzenbucher 1987-1992,*
      Stiftung für Konstructive and Konkrete Kunst, Zürich, Switzerland
   Solo Exhibition, Laura Carpenter Fine Art, Santa Fe, New Mexico
   Solo Exhibition, A/D Gallery, New York, New York
   How It Is, Tony Shafrazi Gallery, New York, New York
   Iconic Abstraction, Rubenstein/Diacono Gallery, New York, New York
   Drawn in the Nineties, curated by Joshua P. Smith, The Katonah Art Gallery,
      Katonah, New York
   Emerging New York Artists, University of Nebraska, Omaha, Nebraska
   Functional Objects by Artists and Architects, Rhona Hoffman Gallery,
      Chicago, Illinois
1991 *Solo Exhibition,* Mario Diacono Gallery, Boston, Massachusetts
   Solo Exhibition, Daniel Weinberg Gallery, Santa Monica, California (also 1990)
1990 *Solo Exhibition,* Simon Watson, New York, New York
   Solo Exhibition (with Moira Dyer), Mario Diacono Gallery, Boston,
      Massachusetts
   Solo Exhibition, University Art Museum, University of California at Berkeley,
      Berkeley, California
   Imagenes de la Abstracción, Fernando Alcolea, Madrid, Spain

Scott Burton

born 1939 in Greensboro, Alabama;
died New York, New York, 1989
1957-1959 studied painting with Leon
Berkowitz, Washington, D.C. and Hans
Hoffman, Provincetown, Massachusetts
1962 BA Columbia University,
New York, New York
1963 MA New York University, New York,
New York

selected recent exhibitions

1993 *Differentes Natures,* LaDefense, Paris, France

1992 *Scott Burton: The Concrete Works,* Max Protech Gallery,
New York, New York

1991 *Scott Burton: The Last Tableau,* Whitney Museum of American Art,
New York, New York

1990 *Scott Burton: Early Works,* Max Protech Gallery, New York, New York
El Sueño de Egipto, El Centro Cultural/Arte Contemporánio,
A. C. Mexico, Ciudad de Mexico, Mexico

1989 *Scott Burton/Sculpturen 1980-89,* Kunstverein für die Rheinlande und
Westfalen, Düsseldorf, West Germany (traveled to Württembergischer
Kunstverein, Stuttgart, West Germany and the Musée des Arts Decoratifs,
Paris, France)
Solo Exhibition Steel Wood Stone, Max Protech Gallery, New York, New York
Prospect '89, Kunstverein, Frankfort, West Germany

1988 *New Chair Sculptures,* Lisson Gallery, London, England
Scott Burton, John C. Stoller & Co., Minneapolis, Minnesota
Rotterdam '88: The City As Stage, Rotterdam, The Netherlands
Furniture As Art: Recent Tendencies in Sculpture, Boymans-van Beuningen
Museum, Rotterdam, The Netherlands
Architectural Art: Affirming the Design Relationship, American Craft Museum,
New York, New York

1987 *Scott Burton,* Max Protech Gallery, New York
Scott Burton, Galerie Rudolf Zwirner, Köln, West Germany
Documenta 8, Kassel, West Germany
Skulptur Projete Münster 1987, Münster, West Germany

1986 *Scott Burton,* Baltimore Museum of Art, Baltimore, Maryland
Solo Exhibition Furniture Sculpture: Recent Geometric Granite Works, Daniel
Weinberg Gallery, Los Angeles, California
Solo Exhibition New Works in Granite and Selected Works in Wood, Max Protech
Gallery, New York, New York
The Museum of Contemporary Art: The Barry Lowen Collection, The Museum of
Contemporary Art, Los Angeles, California

Semi-Circle Table, designed 1988 with fabrication 1989, (edition of 5, 3 prototypes), mild steel

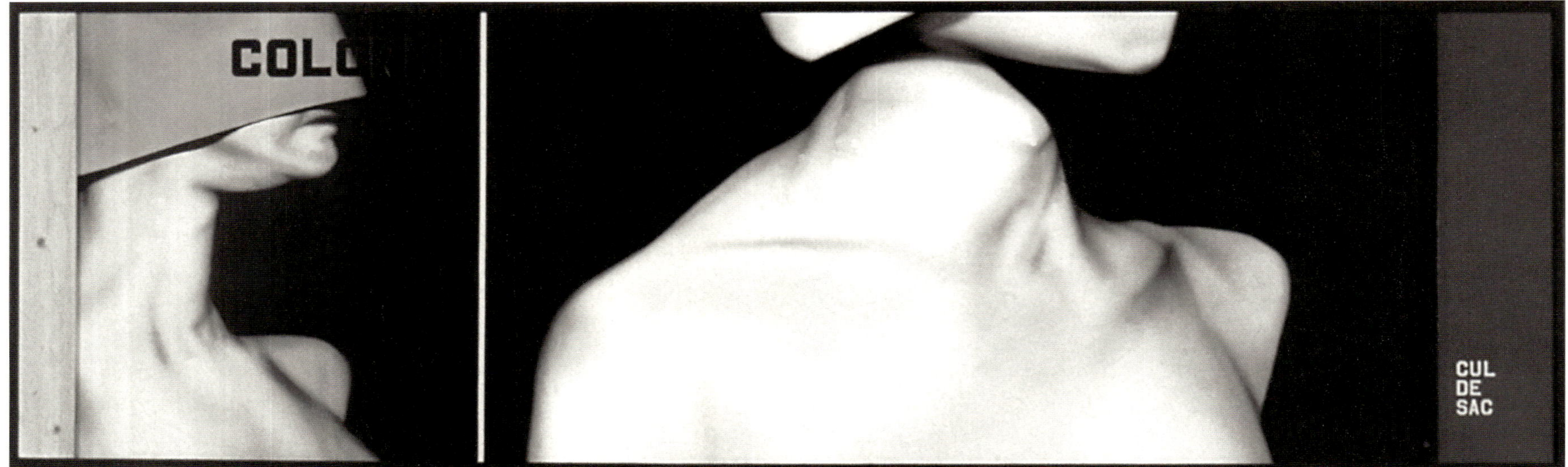

Cul-De-Sac, 1990, ink & enamel on wood

Gerald Lee Cannon

lives in New Orleans, Louisiana
born 1947 in Alexander City, Alabama
1969 BS Auburn University, Auburn, Alabama
1971 MBA Auburn University, Auburn, Alabama
1977 BA (equivalent) University of North Alabama,
  Florence, Alabama
1981 MFA University of New Orleans, New Orleans, Louisiana

selected recent exhibitions

1993 *Painting and Works on Paper-Southern Arts Federation/NEA Fellowship Winners,* Atlanta
  College of Art Gallery, Atlanta, Georgia
1992 *Solo Exhibition, Unfounded Objects,* Still-Zinsel Gallery, New Orleans, Louisiana
  Computer Based Imaging, Galerie Christian Siret, Paris, France and Embassy of the
  United States of America, Bucharest, Hungary
  The Atlantic Richfield Collection, University of Southwestern Louisiana, Lafayette, Louisiana
1991 *Animal Rites and Wrongs,* The University Gallery at Memphis State, Memphis, Tennessee
1990 *Vestiges/Bookworks,* Simms Gallery, New Orleans, Louisiana (traveled)
  Group Show, Space One Eleven, Birmingham, Alabama
  Solo Exhibition, FAMIlies, Still-Zinsel Gallery, New Orleans, Louisiana
1989 *Contemporary Memorials: Hero Building-Vestiges Project,* Contemporary Arts Center,
  New Orleans, Louisiana

selected honors, awards, grants

1992 *Fellowship Recipient,* Louisiana Division of the Arts
  Fellowship Recipient, Southern Arts Federation/NEA, Atlanta, Georgia

Paula Chamlee

lives in Ottsville, Pennsylvania
born 1944 near Adrian, Texas
1970 studied painting with
   Joe C. Michelet
1988 BFA University of South
   Alabama, Mobile, Alabama

selected recent exhibitions

1994 *Natural Connections: Photographs by Paula Chamlee,* Lodima Press, Revere, Pennsylvania
1993 *Winter-Photographs of the Season,* Scott Nichols Gallery, San Francisco, California
   United Artists, Alinder Gallery, Gualala, California
1992 *Prelude to a Portrait of Bucks County* (with Michael A. Smith), James A. Michener Art
   Museum, Doylestown, Pennsylvania
   Bucks Biennial I, James A. Michener Art Museum, Doylestown, Pennsylvania
   The American Landscape, Scott Nichols Gallery, San Francisco, California
1990 *Paula Chamlee: New Work,* The Keepers of Light: A Gallery of Photography, Mobile, Alabama
   Shoot the Earth: Portrait of a Planet Whirling On and *Picture Presents,* Alinder Gallery,
   Gualala, California
1989 *Paula Chamlee: Photographs in Black and White,* Whiting Art Center, Fairhope, Alabama

selected honors, awards, grants

1989 Member of Advisory Board of the American Sport Art Museum and Archives, United States
   Sports Academy, Daphne, Alabama
1986 Member of Board of Advisors for *Art and the Alabama Woman*

Magnetic Hysteresis, 1992, oil on linen

Gary Chapman

lives in Birmingham, Alabama
born 1961 in Xenia, Ohio
1984 BA and BS Berea College, Berea, Kentucky
1986 MFA Cranbrook Academy of Art, Bloomfield Hills, Michigan

selected recent exhibitions

1994 *Solo Exhibition, Anatomy of Reality II,* Durbin Gallery, Birmingham-Southern College, Birmingham, Alabama
Solo Exhibition, Anatomy of Reality, Blue Spiral 1 Gallery, Asheville, North Carolina
Gary Chapman, Sarratt Gallery, Vanderbilt University, Nashville, Tennessee
ARTstravaganza Pavillion Art Exhibition, Chattanooga, Tennessee
Florida National IX, 1994, Florida State University Gallery, Tallahassee, Florida
Images of Faith IV, Blue Spiral 1 Gallery, Asheville, North Carolina
7th National Juried Art Exhibition, Juror Larry M. Walker, Mable Cultural Center, Mableton, Georgia

1993 *Gary Chapman,* Ralston Fine Art, Johnson City, Tennessee
Gary Chapman, University of Alabama at Birmingham Visual Arts Gallery, Birmingham, Alabama
Images of Destruction and Regeneration, VANGUARD Gallery, The Visual Artists Alliance, Nashville, Tennessee (traveled)
New Regional Painting, Moody Gallery of Art, University of Alabama, Tuscaloosa, Alabama
Florida National VIII, 1993, Florida State University Gallery, Tallahassee, Florida
Images of Faith III, Blue Spiral 1 Gallery, Asheville, North Carolina

1992 *Solo Exhibition, The Body and the Spirit,* Bloch Hall Gallery, The University of Montevallo, Montevallo, Alabama
Superstition and Personal Ritual, Fifth Gate Arts Center, Birmingham, Alabama

1991 *Solo Exhibition,* Saint Stephen, The Gallery, Birmingham, Alabama
Tenth Annual, September Competition, Juror, Dennis Barrie, Alexandria Museum of Art, Alexandria, Louisiana

1990 *Artscape '90,* Mount Royal Station Building, Maryland Institute, College of Art, Baltimore, Maryland

1989 *Mysterious Images,* Delaplaine Visual Arts Center, Frederick, Maryland
Solo Exhibition, The Body and the Spirit, Center for the Arts, The Hill School, Pottstown, Pennsylvania

selected honors, awards, grants

1994 *Individual Artist Fellowship Grant,* Alabama State Council on the Arts, Montgomery, Alabama

1993 *Faculty Research Grant,* University of Alabama at Birmingham (also 1991)

1988 *Professional Distinction Award* in *"Maryland's Best," '88,* Juror, Ned Rifkin, Rockland Arts Center, Ellicott City, Maryland

William Christenberry

lives in Washington, D.C.
born 1936 in Tuscaloosa, Alabama
1954 BFA University of Alabama, Tuscaloosa, Alabama
1959 MA University of Alabama, Tuscaloosa, Alabama

selected recent exhibitions

1994 *William Christenberry: A Retrospective,* The Albrecht-Kemper Museum of Art,
St. Joseph, Missouri
William Christenberry, Sculpture and Photographs, Southside Gallery, Oxford, Mississippi
Solo Exhibition, Nancy Drysdale Gallery, Washington, D.C.
House And Home: Spirits of the South, Addison Gallery of American Art, Phillips Academy,
Andover, Massachusetts (traveled)
The Box: From Duchamp to Horn, UBU Gallery, New York, New York
American Studies, The Art Forum Praterinsel, München, Germany
Duchamp's Leg, Walker Art Center, Minneapolis, Minnesota
Worlds in a Box, White Chapel Art Gallery, London, England (Arts Council of Great Britian,
traveled to Edinburgh, Scotland; Norwich and Sheffield, England)
Debut, Kemper Museum of Contemporary Art and Design, Kansas City, Missouri
1993 *William Christenberry,* The Opelika Arts Association, Opelika, Alabama
William Christenberry, Photographs and Sculpture, Ehlers Caudill Gallery, Chicago, Illinois
William Christenberry and Robert Stackhouse, Morgan Gallery, Kansas City, Missouri
Group Exhibition, Southside Gallery, Oxford, Mississippi
1992 *William Christenberry Southern Photographs,* Jackson Fine Art, Inc., Atlanta, Georgia
William Christenberry, Southern Monuments and Dream Buildings, Heath Gallery, Inc.,
Atlanta, Georgia
William Christenberry, Photographs, Huntsville Museum of Art, Huntsville, Alabama
William Christenberry, Photographs and Sculpture, Yellowstone Art Center,
Billings, Montana
William Christenberry, Photographs and Sculpture, Pace/McGill Gallery, New York, New York
William Christenberry, Photographs, Colorado State University, Fort Collins, Colorado
William Christenberry, Southern Views, Moody Gallery, Houston, Texas
William Christenberry, Ethos of the South, Nancy Drysdale Gallery, Washington, D.C.
William Christenberry, Photographs, Tartt Gallery, Washington, D.C.
1991 *William Christenberry,* The Philadelphia Museum of Art, Philadelphia, Pennsylvania
William Christenberry, Millsaps College, Jackson, Mississippi
William Christenberry, Austin College, Sherman, Texas
Solo Exhibition, Thirty by Forty Photographs, Middendorf Gallery, Washington, D.C.
The Southern Landscape, Morris Museum of Art, Augusta, Georgia
Eadweard Muybridge and Contemporary American Photography, National Museum of
American Art, Washington, D.C. (traveled)
Group Exhibition, Nancy Drysdale Gallery, Washington, D.C.
Southern Grit, The Tartt Gallery, Washington, D.C.

selected honors, awards, grants

1994 *Art Matters Grant,* New York, New York
1993 *Visiting Artist,* Yale University Summer School of Art and Music, Norfolk, Connecticut
(also 1991)
Eudora Welty Professor of Southern Studies, Spring Semester, Millsaps College,
Jackson, Mississippi
1989 *The Alabama Prize,* The Tuscaloosa News, Florence Times Daily, and The Gadsden Times

Clan Dolls, 1992, EK 74 photograph

Stairwell, Barton Hall (ca. 1847), 1993, cibachrome print

Chip Cooper

lives in Tuscaloosa, Alabama
born 1949 in Savannah, Georgia
1972 BA University of Alabama, Tuscaloosa, Alabama
1972-1973 Post-graduate work in photography,
　　University of Alabama, Tuscaloosa, Alabama

selected recent exhibitions

1993　*Solo Exhibition, Silent in the Land,* Fay Gold Gallery, Atlanta, Georgia and The
　　　State Capitol, Montgomery, Alabama
　　　Art Forms and Messages, The Partnership Gallery, Montgomery, Alabama
　　　Silent in the Land, CKM Press, Tuscaloosa, Alabama
1992　*Encounters 19: Chip Cooper,* The Huntsville Museum of Art, Huntsville, Alabama
1991　*Solo Exhibition Alabama Memories,* Centro Cultural Costarricense Nordamericano,
　　　San Jose, Costa Rica
　　　Solo Exhibition Alabama Memories, Instituto Guatamala Americano, Guatamala City,
　　　Guatemala (traveled)
1990　*Black and White and Color,* Center for Cultural Arts, Gadsden, Alabama
1989　*In View of Home: Alabama Landscape Photographs,* Huntsville Museum of Art,
　　　Huntsville, Alabama (traveled)
　　　Alabama Memories, Gallery Books, W.H. Smith Publishers, Inc. New York, New York

selected honors, awards, grants

1994　*Award of Excellence, Book Series 1994,* Communication Arts Magazine; selected for
　　　inclusion in "Communication Arts 1994 Photography Annual" and the
　　　"1994 Print Magazine Regional Design Annual "
　　　Awards, University Press Photographers Association, Washington, D.C.

Suzan Courtney

lives in New York, New York
born 1947 in Mobile, Alabama
1968-1969 Tulane University College,
   New Orleans, Louisiana
1973 Diploma in Art and Design, Kingston-Upon-Hull
   College of Art, Hull, England
1974-1975 Whitney Museum of American Art
   Independent Study Program, New York, New York
1977 MFA Yale University School of Art,
   New Haven, Connecticut

selected recent exhibitions

1992   *Solo Exhibition,* Galerie Gordon Pym et Fils, Paris, France
   Europa-America 360 E-Venti, Pino Molica Gallery, New York, New York
   Miauhaus Exhibition, Thread Waxing Space, New York, New York
1991   *Drawing Show,* Parsons School of Design, New York, New York
1990   *Solo Exhibition,* Gasperi Gallery, New Orleans, Louisiana

selected honors, awards, grants

1980   *Residency Fellowship,* Edward Albee Foundation, Mountauk, New York

Circular XXXV, 1994, fabricated bronze

Casey Downing, Jr.

lives in Mobile, Alabama
born 1948 in Tuscaloosa, Alabama
1971 University of South Alabama,
   Mobile, Alabama
1976 BA University of Alabama at Huntsville,
   Huntsville, Alabama
Studied sculpture with Jude Johnston and
   Jimmie Dawkins

selected recent exhibitions

1994 *3-D in 94,* National Sculpture Exhibition, Juror, David Collins, Middletown
    Arts Center, New York, New York
    Red Clay Survey; Fourth Biennial Exhibition of Contemporary Southern Art,
    Huntsville Museum of Art, Huntsville, Alabama
    Group Exhibition, Bill Bace Gallery, New York
    Outdoor Installation, Henri Gallery, Washington, D.C.
1993 *Solo Exhibition,* Henri Gallery, Washington, D.C.
1992 *Casey Downing: Recent Works,* Tacon Station Gallery, Mobile, Alabama
1991 *Outdoor Sculpture Display,* University of Alabama at Birmingham,
    Birmingham, Alabama (through 1993)
    Showcase II, Alabama State Council on the Arts Gallery, Montgomery, Alabama
1990 *Twenty Sculptors,* Henri Gallery, Washington, D.C.
    Group Show, Maralyn Wilson Gallery, Birmingham, Alabama
1989 *Group Show,* Novus Gallery, Atlanta, Georgia
    Solo Exhibition, Fine Arts Museum of the South, Mobile, Alabama

selected honors, awards, grants

1994 *Individual Artist Fellowship Grant,* Alabama State Council on the Arts,
    Montgomery, Alabama
1991 *Purchase Award,* Outdoor Sculpture Display, University of Alabama at
    Birmingham, Birmingham, Alabama

Wounded Heart, 1994, glazed white earthenware

Alice Hohenberg Federico

lives in New York, New York
born 1945 in Selma, Alabama
1967 BA Hollins College, Roanoke,
 North Carolina
1977 MFA East Carolina University,
 Greenville, North Carolina
1983 BFA Kansas City Art Institute,
 Kansas City, Missouri

selected recent exhibitions

1993 *Recent Works,* Cortland Jessup Gallery, Provincetown, Massachusetts
 Recent Works, Siegel Gallery, Selma, Alabama (also 1989)
1992 *Solo Exhibition,* Monty Stabler Galleries, Birmingham, Alabama (also 1991)
 Biennale Internationale de Céramique, Vallauris, France
 Fletcher Challenge, Auckland, New Zealand
1991 *Feats of Clay IV,* Lincoln Arts, Lincoln, California
 New Visions: Forms with Function, Northfield, Illinois
 Greater Midwest Invitational, Warrensberg, Missouri
1990 *The 28th Ceramic National Exhibition,* Everson Museum of Art, Syracuse, New York
 Recent Works, Bronx River Art Gallery, Bronx, New York
 Recent Works, The Clay Studio, Philadelphia, Pennsylvania
1989 *International Ceramics Competition,* Mino, Japan
 Recent Works, Usdan Gallery, Bennington College, Bennington, Vermont

Parrot Chair, 1980, cast bronze

Frank Fleming

lives in Birmingham, Alabama
born 1940 in Bear Creek, Alabama
1962 BS Florence State College, Florence, Alabama
1969 MA University of Alabama, Tuscaloosa, Alabama
1973 MFA University of Alabama, Tuscaloosa, Alabama

selected recent exhibitions

1994   *Solo Exhibition,* Galerie Simonne Stern, New Orleans, Louisiana (also 1991)
  Summer Gallery Show, Heath Gallery, Atlanta, Georgia
  Sculpture South 94, South Carolina State Museum of Art, Columbia, South Carolina
  Alabama Crafts, Alabama State Council on the Arts Gallery, Montgomery, Alabama
  Small Sculpture, Elaine Horwitch Gallery, Scottsdale, Arizona
1993   *Solo Exhibition,* Robert Kidd Gallery, Birmingham, Michigan (also 1990)
  Solo Exhibition, Kentuck Museum, Northport, Alabama
  Solo Exhibition, Moody Gallery, Houston, Texas
  Outdoor Sculpture, Gwinnett Cultural Center, Atlanta, Georgia (thru 1994)
  Fur, Fins, Feathers, and More, Galveston Arts Center, Galveston, Texas
  Fantastical Art with Wit, Wiregrass Museum of Art, Dothan, Alabama
  Sculpture, Martha Maybey Gallery, Richmond, Virginia
  Just Like Us, Skyharbor Airport, Phoenix, Arizona
1992   *Solo Exhibition,* Morgan Gallery, Kansas City, Missouri
  Solo Exhibition, Elaine Horwitch Gallery, Santa Fe, New Mexico
  American Crafts-The Nation's Collection, Renwick Gallery, National Museum of
    American Art, Smithsonian Institution, Washington, D.C.
  The Archives of American Art Mailbox Exhibition, Detroit, Michigan
  Recent Works, Kathryn Fleck Gallery, Aspen, Colorado
1991   *Keepers of the Kiln,* Morgan Gallery, Kansas City, Missouri (traveled)
  A Beastly Exhibition, South Bend Arts Center, South Bend, Indiana
  Fourth International Shoe Box Sculpture Exhibition, University of Hawaii Gallery,
    Honolulu, Hawaii (traveled)
1990   *Solo Exhibition,* Elaine Horwitch Gallery, Palm Springs, California
  American Figurative Ceramics, National Museum of American Ceramics,
    Baltimore, Maryland
  Fin, Fur, and Feather, Laguna Gloria Art Museum, Austin, Texas
  Southeast Figurative Ceramics, Louisiana State University Gallery,
    Baton Rouge, Louisiana

selected honors, awards, grants

1988   *Fellowship Recipient,* Southern Arts Federation/NEA, Atlanta, Georgia

Maud Gatewood

lives in Yanceyville, North Carolina
born 1934 in Yanceyville, North Carolina
1954 BA Woman's College of University
 of North Carolina, Greensboro,
 North Carolina
1955 MA The Ohio State University,
 Columbus, Ohio
Taught Huntingdon College, Montgomery,
 Alabama, 1956-1958

selected recent exhibitions

1994 *Maud Gatewood Re-Visions,* Weatherspoon Art Gallery, The University of North
 Carolina at Greensboro, Greensboro, North Carolina (traveled)
1993 *Solo Exhibition,* Somerhill Gallery, Chapel Hill, North Carolina (also 1991)
1992 *Maud Gatewood: Works on Paper,* Green Hill Center for North Carolina Art,
 Greensboro, North Carolina
 Solo Exhibition, In Celebration (Centennial of UNC at Greensboro),
 Weatherspoon Art Gallery, The University of North Carolina at Greensboro
 National Contemporary Painting Competition, Cheekwood Museum of Art,
 Nashville, Tennessee
1991 *New Regional Painting,* University of Alabama, Tuscaloosa, Alabama

selected honors, awards, grants

1984 *Governor's Award,* North Carolina Award in Fine Arts
 Alumni Service Award, University of North Carolina at Greensboro, Greensboro,
 North Carolina

Snow and Wind, 1977, acrylic on canvas

Burning Landscape, 1994, cibachrome II print

Joseph W. Gluhman

lives in Auburn, Alabama
born 1934 in Corpus Christi, Texas
1955 AB Johns Hopkins University,
   Baltimore, Maryland
1962 MA Western Reserve University,
   Cleveland, Ohio
1970 PhD Harvard University,
   Cambridge, Massachusetts

selected recent exhibitions

1994 *Solo Exhibition, Transformations: Recent Photographs,* Wiregrass
   Museum of Art, Dothan, Alabama
   Henley Southeastern Spectrum 1994, Associated Artists Galleries,
   Winston-Salem, North Carolina
   12th National Maine/Maritime Flatworks Exhibition, University of
   Maine-Presque Isle, Maine (also 1993 and 1991)
   Annual Bi-State Art Competition, Meridian Museum of Art, Meridian,
   Mississippi (also 1993, 1992, and 1991)
   Wiregrass Biennial Art Competition, Wiregrass Museum of Art, Dothan,
   Alabama (also 1993, 1992, and 1990)

1993 *Joseph W. Gluhman: Recent Photographs,* Meridian Museum of Art,
   Meridian, Mississippi
   21st Annual Exhibition South '93, Tennessee Valley Art Center,
   Tuscumbia, Alabama
   Art with a Southern Drawl, University of Mobile, Mobile, Alabama
   (also 1992)
   Greater Midwest International Exhibition VIII, Central Missouri State
   University, Warrensburg, Missouri

1992 *6th Annual North Florida Juried Art Competition,* Florida State
   University, Tallahassee, Florida (also 1990)

1991 *Counterpoint: National Juried Exhibition,* Hill Country Arts Foundation,
   Ingram, Texas
   Border to Border/Larson National Biennial Drawing Competition,
   Trahern Gallery, Austin Peay State University, Clarksville, Tennessee
   LaGrange National XVI, Chattahochee Valley Art Museum and Lamar
   Dodd Art Center, LaGrange College, LaGrange, Georgia
   Flying Colors Invitational Exhibition, Columbus Museum,
   Columbus, Georgia
   Southern Facades, Etc., CNN Center, Atlanta, Georgia

1990 *New Works/New Alabamians,* Foy Union Gallery, Auburn University,
   Auburn, Alabama (traveled)
   Midwest Photography Invitational VI, University of Wisconsin-Green Bay,
   Green Bay, Wisconsin (traveled)
   The Halpert Biennial Juried Competition, Appalachian State University,
   Boone, North Carolina
   Southeastern '90 Juried Exhibition, Fine Arts Museum of the South,
   Mobile, Alabama

Guy Goodwin

lives in New York, New York
born 1940 in Birmingham, Alabama
1963 BFA Auburn University,
  Auburn, Alabama
1965 MFA University of Illinois,
  Champaign-Urbana, Illinois

Membrane, 1991, oil on linen

selected recent exhibitions

1993 *Group Exhibition,* Susanne Hilberry Gallery, Birmingham, Michigan
  Skowhegan '93, Colby College Museum of Art, Waterville, Maine
1991 *Solo Exhibition,* Susanne Hilberry Gallery, Birmingham, Michigan
  New Currents in Watercolor, The Noyes Museum, Oceanville, New Jersey
  Collector's Exhibition, Arkansas Arts Center, Little Rock, Arkansas
  1991 Invitational, New Britain Museum of American Art, New Britain, Connecticut
  Drawings, Susanne Hilberry Gallery, Birmingham, Michigan
1990 *Solo Exhibition,* Dolan/Maxwell Gallery, New York, New York
  Guy Goodwin New Paintings, Wetterling Gallery, Göteborg, Sweden
  Group Exhibition, Dolan/Maxwell Gallery, New York, New York
  Waterworks, ULAE, New York, New York
1989 *Solo Exhibition,* Dolan/Maxwell Gallery, New York, New York
  A Decade of American Drawings, Daniel Weinberg Gallery, Santa Monica, California
  Tools As Art, The Heckinger Collection, National Building Museum, Washington, D.C.
  Group Show, Dolan/Maxwell Gallery, Philadelphia, Pennsylvania

selected honors, awards, grants

1994 *Individual Support Grant,* Adolph and Esther Gottlieb Foundation, New York, New York
1992 *Fellowship Recipient,* John Simon Guggenheim Memorial Foundation, New York, New York
1989 *Board of Governors,* Skowhegan School of Painting and Sculpture, Skowhegan, Maine
1980 *Fellowship Recipient,* National Endowment for the Arts, Washington, D.C.

Solar Cuts, 1988, acrylic on wood

Gerald Hayes

lives in New York, New York
born 1940 in Los Angeles, California
1962 BA Auburn University,
   Auburn, Alabama
1966 MA University of Illinois,
   Champaign-Urbana, Illinois

selected recent exhibitions

1990 *Solo Exhibition,* Stockton State College Gallery, Pomona, New Jersey
      Solo Exhibition, Calkins Gallery, Hofstra University, Hempstead, New York
1986 *Small Scale Abstraction,* Grace Borgenicht Gallery, New York, New York
1985 *New Works by Hays, Miller, Ortwein,* Pyramid Arts Center, Rochester, New York
      Invitational, Biggin Hall Art Gallery, Auburn University, Auburn, Alabama
1984 *New Jersey Arts Inclusion Program,* Jane Voorhees Zimmerli Art Museum,
      Rutgers University, New Brunswick, New Jersey
1983 *Newcastle Salutes New York,* Newcastle Polytechnic Art Gallery,
      Newcastle, England

selected honors, awards, grants

1993 *Juror,* Individual Artist Grants, Painting and Graphics Jury, New Jersey State
      Council on the Arts, Trenton, New Jersey (1992 and 1991)

Cham Hendon

lives in Brooklyn, New York
born 1936 in Birmingham, Alabama
1958 BS Georgia Institute of Technology,
  Atlanta, Georgia
1963 BFA School of the Art Institute of Chicago,
  Chicago, Illinois
1965 MA University of New Mexico, Albuquerque,
  New Mexico
1977 MFA University of Wisconsin-Madison,
  Madison, Wisconsin

selected recent exhibitions

1994 *Solo Exhibition,* Monty Stabler Galleries, Birmingham, Alabama
  (1993, 1992, 1991, and 1990)
  Tandem Press: Five Years of Collaboration and Experimentation, Elvehjem Museum
    of Art, University of Wisconsin-Madison, Madison, Wisconsin
1993 *Solo Exhibition,* Columbia-Greene Community College, Hudson, New York
1992 *Solo Exhibition,* The Red Mills, Claverack, New York (Merchant-Ivory Foundation)
  Admiration and Esteem: Peter Dean Is Honored by His Friends, G.W. Einstein Gallery,
    New York, New York
1991 *Solo Exhibition,* Moody Gallery, University of Alabama, Tuscaloosa, Alabama
  *American Narrative Painting and Sculpture, The 1980's: Selections from the Collection
    of The Metropolitan Museum of Art,* Nassau County Museum of Art, Roslyn Harbor,
    New York
1990 *Solo Exhibition,* Gallery of Art, University of Northern Iowa, Cedar Falls, Iowa
  Solo Exhibition, The Waterworks Visual Arts Center, Salisbury, North Carolina
1989 *Solo Exhibition,* Gray Art Gallery, East Carolina University, Greenville, North Carolina
1987 *Solo Exhibition,* Phyllis Kind Gallery, New York, New York
  39th Annual Purchase Exhibition, American Academy and Institute of Arts and Letters,
    New York, New York

Bessy, 1994, acrylic on canvas

1990-II, 1990, stainless steel, aluminum, painted brass, gold leaf, level

Edward Lee Hendricks

lives in Sagaponack, New York
born 1952 in Charleston, West Virginia;
    resided Birmingham, Alabama 1960-1990
1974 BFA Birmingham-Southern College,
    Birmingham, Alabama
1976 MFA University of North Carolina at
    Chapel Hill, Chapel Hill, North Carolina

selected recent exhibitions

1994 *Solo Exhibition,* Eve Mannes Gallery, Atlanta, Georgia
1993 *Solo Exhibition,* Brendan Walter Gallery, Los Angeles, California
    Solo Exhibition, Louis K. Meisel Gallery, New York, New York
1992 *Solo Exhibition,* Arden Gallery, Boston, Massachusetts
1991 *Solo Exhibition,* Eve Mannes Gallery, Atlanta, Georgia
    Solo Exhibition, Elaine Horwitch Gallery, Scottsdale, Arizona
1990 *Solo Exhibition,* de Andino Fine Arts, Washington, D.C.
    Solo Exhibition, Elaine Horwitch Gallery, Palm Springs, California (also 1988)
    Solo Exhibition, Brendan Walter Gallery, Los Angeles, California
1989 *Solo Exhibition,* Alexander F. Milliken, Inc., New York, New York
    Solo Exhibition, Eva Cohon Gallery, Chicago, Illinois
    Birmingham Artists: 1959-1989, Birmingham Museum of Art, Birmingham, Alabama
1988 *Looking South: A Different Dixie,* Birmingham Museum of Art, Birmingham, Alabama
    (traveled)
    In Large Scale, Arden Gallery, Boston, Massachusetts
    Exhibition of Gallery Artists, Alexander F. Milliken, Inc., New York, New York

selected honors, awards, grants

1982 *Fellowship Recipient,* Southern Arts Federation/NEA, Atlanta, Georgia
1979 *Juror's Award,* Juror, Dennis Oppenheim, "*Birmingham Art Association,*"
    Birmingham, Alabama
1975 *Second Award, "National Sculpture '75,"* Juror, Stephen Antonakos, Huntsville
    Museum of Art, Huntsville, Alabama

Chester Higgins, Jr.

lives in Brooklyn, New York
born 1946 in Kentucky; since infancy
resided New Brockton, Alabama, 1946-1970
1970 BS Tuskegee Institute, Tuskegee, Alabama

selected recent exhibitions

1994 *Solo Exhibition, Invoking the Spirit: Worship Traditions in the African World,* Schomburg
     Center for Research in Black Culture/New York Public Library, New York, New York
     Feeling The Spirit: Searching the World for the People of Africa, Bantam Books,
     New York, New York
1993 *From the Permanent Collection,* Museum of Modern Art, New York, New York
1980 *Group Exhibition, The Official Cabinet Portraits of the Carter Administration,* The
     National Portrait Gallery, Washington, D.C.
     *Some Time Ago (*with Orde Coombs), Doubleday/Anchor Press, New York, New York
1979 *Solo Exhibition,* Wellesley College, Wellesley, Massachusetts
1978 *Solo Exhibition,* U.S. Department of Housing and Urban Development, Washington, D.C.
1974 *Solo Exhibition, Acts* of Art Gallery, New York, New York
     *Drums of Life (*with Orde Coombs), Doubleday/Anchor Press, New York, New York

Life of the Soul, 1994, iris print on watercolor paper

Jackson Hill

lives in New Orleans, Louisiana
born 1949 in Greensboro, North Carolina;
resided Mobile, Alabama 1951-1976

selected recent exhibitions

1994 *New Orleans Photographers,* Sylvia Schmidt Gallery, New Orleans, Louisiana
1991 *Solo Exhibition, W. B. Yeats' Ireland,* Hotel Intercontinental, New Orleans, Louisiana
1984 *Solo Exhibition,* Fine Arts Museum of the South, Mobile, Alabama
1978 *On Mobile Streets, A Rumor of the City,* Easter Publishing Company, Mobile, Alabama

Nall Hollis (Nall)

lives in Vence, France
born 1948 in Troy, Alabama
1970 BA University of Alabama,
    Tuscaloosa, Alabama
attended L'Ecole des Beaux-Arts, Paris,
    France (studied with Lucien Coutaud)

selected recent exhibitions

1994 *Nall's New Orientalism,* Gallery Mouvances, Paris, France
    Details and Essence of Nall's New Orientalism, Monaco Fine Art Gallery,
        Monte-Carlo, Monaco
    Nall au Pays des Merveilles (Arts en Amerique), Palais des Congres Europa,
        Mandelieu, France
    Group Exhibition, Musée d'Art Moderne et d'Art Contemporain,
        Nice, France
    Group Exhibition, La Pittura e la Scultura Fatastica e Visionaria, Museo
        "Le Zittelle," Venice, Italy
    Group Exhibition, Mistral Galleries, London, England
1993 *Solo Exhibition, Sensuality and Other Vanities,* Chapelle Sainte Elizabeth,
        Musée de la citadelle de Villefranche, Villefranche, France
    Nall's New Orientalism, UNISYS, Saint Paul de Vence, France
    Group Exhibition, Chateau de Cagnes sur Mer, Cagnes, France (also 1992)
    Group Exhibition, Autoportraits, Unisys, Saint-Paul de Vence, France
    Group Exhibition, Festival des Arts, Beaulieu sur Mer, France
    Group Exhibition, Fondation Santé des Etudiants de France, Vence, France
1992 *Nall: A Retrospective 1976-1992,* Abela Hotel, Nice, France
    Group Exhibition, Gallery Rosa Lopez, Vence, France
    Group Exhibition, Maison des Artistes du Vieu Bourg, France
1991 *Solo Exhibition,* Relais Socio-Culturel Peirese, Toulon, France
    Solo Exhibition, Gallery Henry, Pau, France
    Solo Exhibition, Museum of Saint Paul, Saint-Paul, France
    Solo Exhibition, Museum of Sainte-Maxime, Saint-Maxime, France
    Solo Exhibition, Centre of Contemporary Art, Valbonne, France
    Solo Exhibition, Gallery Place des Arts, Vallauris, France
    Group Exhibition Festival of Arts, Beaulieu-sur-Mer, France
    Group Exhibition, Peintre du Pays Vencois, Lahnstein, Germany
1990 *Solo Exhibition,* Gallery Touraj, Monte-Carlo, Monaco
    Solo Exhibition, Gallery Orcades, Cannes, France
    Solo Exhibition, Centre Culturel Henri Matisse, Vence, France

Portrait of Sheree, 1990-1994, mixed media

Bill & Neils, Phenix City, 1993, acrylic & varnish on canvas

Mike Howard

lives in Brooklyn, New York
born 1944 in Phenix City, Alabama
1968-1971 University of Georgia,
    Athens, Georgia
1969-1970 Whitney Museum of
    American Art Independent Study
    Program, New York, New York
1972 BS Columbus College,
    Columbus, Georgia
1975 MFA Rutgers University,
    New Brunswick, New Jersey

selected recent exhibitions

1993 *Solo Exhibition,* Jason Rubell Gallery, Palm Beach, Florida
    Group Exhibition, Jason Rubell Gallery, Miami, Florida
    Group Exhibition, Hall-Barnett Gallery, New Orleans, Louisiana
        (also 1992, 1991, 1990, 1989, and 1988)
1992 *Boy Meets Girl,* Horodner Romley Gallery, New York, New York
    10 Steps, Horodner Romley Gallery, New York, New York
1991 *Solo Exhibition,* Baby Doll Lounge, New York, New York
    J.F.K., Rene Fotouhi Fine Art, East Hampton, New York
    J.F.K., B4A Gallery, New York, New York
1990 *Home Again,* Columbus Museum, Columbus, Georgia
1989 *Solo Exhibition,* Hall-Barnett Gallery, New Orleans, Louisiana
1988 *Billboards,* Little John Smith, New York, New York
    Art and Law, Metropolitan Toronto Convention Center, Toronto,
        Ontario, Canada
    The Flower Show, Betsy Rosenfield Gallery, Chicago, Illinois
    Situations, Museum of Modern Art Advisory Service, General
        Electric Corporation, Fairfield, Connecticut
    Products and Promotion, Franklin Furnace, New York
    Fish Show, Brent Gallery, Houston, Texas
1988 *Manhattan Painting Show,* Baum School of Art, Allentown,
        Pennsylvania
1987 *Solo Exhibition,* Gracie Mansion Gallery, New York, New York
    Solo Exhibition, Art & Exhibit, Ltd., New York, New York
    Mike Howard, Survey of Paintings 1979-1986, Jane Voorhees
        Zimmerli Art Museum, Rutgers University, New Brunswick,
        New Jersey

selected honors, awards, grants

1991 *Individual Support Grant,* Adolph and Esther Gottlieb
        Foundation, New York, New York
    Individual Grant, Pollock-Krasner Foundation, New York,
        New York
    Fellowship Recipient, New York Arts and Letters Foundation,
        New York, New York
1985 *Grant* (for Studio Space at P.S. 1), National Endowment for
        the Arts, Washington, D.C.

Steven Bernard Jones

lives in Austin, Texas
born 1961 in Houston, Texas;
   resided Auburn, Alabama 1966-1980
1986 BFA University of Florida,
   Gainesville, Florida
1990 MFA The University of Texas at
   Austin, Austin, Texas

selected recent exhibitions

1994 *Group Exhibition,* Project Row Houses, Houston, Texas
   I Remember, Blaffer Gallery, University of Houston, Houston, Texas
1993 *In Response To Nature,* Laguna Gloria Art Museum, Austin, Texas
   The Greatest Show On Earth, Niendorff Art Gallery, Austin, Texas
   UT Faculty Show, Archer M. Huntington Art Gallery, The University of
      Texas at Austin, Austin, Texas
   Blacks and Whites Together, Barnes-Blackman Gallery, Houston, Texas
   Individual Ideologies, Hickory Street Gallery, Dallas, Texas
1992 *Fresh Visions, New Voices,* The Glassell School of Art, The Museum of Fine Arts,
      Houston, Texas (traveled to Galveston Museum of Fine Art, Galveston, Texas and
      Arlington Museum of Art, Arlington, Texas)
   Counter Colon-ialismo Exhibition, Diverse Works Artspace, Houston, Texas (traveled to
      MARS Art Space and The Heard Museum, Phoenix, Arizona; Centro Cutural de la Raza,
      San Diego, California; Mexic-Arte Museum, Austin, Texas; Galeria Posada and Center for
      Contemporary Art, Sacramento, California; and Centro Cultural Tijuana, Tijuana, Mexico)
1991 *Group Exhibition,* Stupid Art Gallery of America, Austin, Texas
1990 *Installation,* Ruby's B.B.Q., Austin, Texas

selected honors, awards, grants

1992 *Honorarium,* Glassell School of Art, The Museum of Fine Arts, Houston, Texas
   Honorarium, Jumpstart Theatre, San Antonio, Texas
1991 *Grant,* New Forms Regional Initiative Grant (NFRIG)
   Honorarium, Mexic-Arte Museum, Austin, Texas; Diverse Works Artspace, Houston, Texas,
      and the National Endowment for the Arts, Washington, D.C. for *Counter Colon-ialismo.*
   Grant, Franklin Furnace Performance Grant, New York, New York, funded by the Jerome
      Foundation, Inc., St. Paul, Minnasota

Holy Annihilation, 1993, mixed media

Contemporary Frieze, 1994, oil on canvas

Dale Kennington

lives in Dothan, Alabama
born 1935 in Savannah, Georgia
1956 BA University of Alabama, Tuscaloosa, Alabama
1958 post-graduate work, Auburn University,
   Auburn, Alabama

selected recent exhibitons

1994 *Dale Kennington: Time and Place,* (organized by the Wiregrass Museum of Art,
   Dothan, Alabama; traveled to Louisiana Arts and Science Center, Baton Rouge,
   Louisiana; Davidson College Art Gallery, Davidson, North Carolina; R.S. Barnwell
   Art Center, Shreveport, Louisiana; Auburn University Art Gallery, Auburn, Alabama)
   Solo Exhibition, Linda McAdoo Galleries, Santa Fe, New Mexico
   58th Annual Mid-year Show, Butler Institute of American Art, Youngstown, Ohio
   Chiaroscuro: A Contemporary Study of Light and Dark, Montgomery Museum of
   Fine Arts, Montgomery, Alabama
   The Red Clay Survey: Fourth Biennial Exhibition of Contemporary Southern Art,
   Huntsville Museum of Art, Huntsville, Alabama
   Alabama Signatures, Alabama State Council on the Arts Gallery, Montgomery, Alabama
   Visual Voices: The Female, Art Gallery of the University of West Florida,
   Pensacola, Florida
   National Contemporary Painting Competition, Cheekwood Museum of Art,
   Nashville, Tennessee
   Group Exhibtion, Gadsden Center of Cultural Arts, Gadsden, Alabama
   Group Exhibition, Malone Gallery, Troy State University, Troy, Alabama

1993 *Solo Exhibition,* Kennedy-Douglass Center for the Arts, Florence, Alabama
   57th Annual Mid-year Show, Butler Institute of American Art, Youngstown, Ohio
   Southeastern Juried Exhibition 1993, Juror, Henry Hopkins, Fine Arts Museum
   of the South, Mobile, Alabama
   Alabama Contemporary Women Artists Exhibition, Alabama State Council on the
   Arts Gallery, Montgomery, Alabama
   Faber Birren Watercolor Award Show, Stamford, Connecticut
   Group Exhibition, Wiregrass Museum of Art, Dothan, Alabama
   Group Exhibition, Whiting Art Center, Fairhope, Alabama

1992 *Solo Exhibition,* Visual Arts Center of Northwest Florida, Panama City, Florida
   Solo Exhibition, Evelyn Bengston Gallery, Greensboro, North Carolina
   Solo Exhibition, Loretta Goodwin Gallery, Birmingham, Alabama

1991 *Solo Exhibition,* Wiregrass Museum of Art, Dothan, Alabama
   Solo Exhibition, Green Garden Gallery, Birmingham, Alabama (also 1990)
   Group Exhibition, Swan Coach House Gallery, Atlanta, Georgia

Janice Kluge

Then She Was Gone, 1991, wood, metal, & sandblasted glass

lives in Birmingham, Alabama
born 1952 in Berwyn, Illinois
1974 BFA University of Illinois,
  Champaign-Urbana, Illinois
1980 MA University of Wisconsin-
  Madison, Madison, Wisconsin
1982 MFA University of Wisconsin-
  Madison, Madison, Wisconsin

selected recent exhibitions

1994 *Group Exhibition,* Blackfish Gallery, Portland, Oregon
1993 *Exploring Metals,* Maralyn Wilson Gallery, Birmingham, Alabama
1992 *Silver Jubilee,* John Michael Kohler Arts Center, Sheboygan, Wisconsin
  Master Metalsmiths, The Hand and the Spirit Gallery, Scottsdale, Arizona
1991 *Invitational Exhibition,* Heartworks Gallery, Jacksonville, Florida
  Group Exhibition, Personal Metaphors, Connell Gallery/Great American
    Gallery, Atlanta, Georgia
1990 *Fellowship Winners' Exhibition,* Alabama State Council on the Arts Gallery,
    Montgomery, Alabama
  Focus Four Alabama Artists, Birmingham Museum of Art, Birmingham, Alabama
1988 *Blue Angel,* A.I.R. Gallery, New York, New York
  Lilliputians, Southeastern Center for Contemporary Art, Winston-Salem,
    North Carolina

selected honors, awards, grants

1992 *Environmental Play Sculpture,* City of Birmingham, Alabama
1988 *Individual Artist Grant,* Alabama State Council on the Arts,
    Montgomery, Alabama
  Interdisciplinary Research Grant, Environmental Play Sculpture, School
    of Education, University of Alabama at Birmingham, Birmingham, Alabama
1987 *Faculty Research Grant, The Investigation of Color as a Means to Alter
    Perception in Sculpture,* University of Alabama at Birmingham,
    Birmingham, Alabama

Red Bouquet, 1985, blown glass

Cam Langley

lives in Birmingham, Alabama
born 1948 in Norfolk, Virginia
1970 BS Virginia Polytechnic Institute and
   State University, Blacksburg, Virginia
1979 Penland School of Crafts, Penland,
   North Carolina
1979-1982, University of Wisconsin-Madison,
   Madison, Wisconsin

selected recent exhibitions

1993 *Cam Langley, Glass,* Ariodante, New Orleans, Louisiana (also 1992)
1992 *Glass Invitational 1992,* Ariana Gallery, Birmingham, Michigan
   Down the Garden Path, Contemporary Crafts Association, Portland, Oregon
   Beauties and Beasts: Issues of Aesthetics, Space One Eleven, Birmingham,
      Michigan
1991 *Glass Invitational,* Design Concepts Galleries, Orleans, Massachusetts
   Group Exhibition, Maralyn Wilson Gallery, Birmingham, Alabama
   Group Exhibition, Balcony Gallery, Berlin, Maryland
   Flowers, Fruits and Vegetables, Ariodante Gallery, New Orleans
1990 *Southwest Glass Invitational,* Philabaum Glass Gallery, Tuscon, Arizona
   Annual Invitational, Naples Art Gallery, Naples, Florida
   Chalice Show, Connell Gallery/Great American Gallery, Atlanta, Georgia
   Trends in Contemporary Photography and Glass, Meridian Museum of Art,
      Meridian, Mississippi
   Glass in Black and White, Grand Avenue Frame and Gallery, St. Paul, Minnesota
   Spring Ahead: Flowers Forseen, Elizabeth Fortner Gallery, Santa Barbara,
      California

selected honors, awards, grants

1981 *Apprentice Fellowship in Crafts,* National Endowment for the Arts,
   Washington, D.C.

Frances de La Rosa

lives in Uniontown, Alabama
born 1958 in Selma, Alabama
1980 BA University of Alabama,
  Tuscaloosa, Alabama
1984 MFA Tulane University,
  New Orleans, Louisiana

selected recent exhibitions

1993   *Solo Exhibition,* Sandler Hudson Gallery, Atlanta, Georgia (also 1991)
       Solo Exhibition, Gallery 1024, Birmingham, Alabama (also 1990)
1991   *The Power of Scale: Works in Miniature by Eight Contemporary Artists,*
         Art Museum of South Texas, Corpus Christi, Texas
       Southern Arts Federation Award Recipients, Atlanta College of Art Gallery,
         Atlanta, Georgia (traveled)
1992   *Solo Exhibition,* Galerie Simonne Stern, New Orleans, Louisiana (also 1990)
       Group Exhibition, Fine Art Alumni, Auburn University Art Gallery,
         Auburn, Alabama
1989   *Solo Exhibition,* Alice Bingham Gallery, Memphis, Tennessee
1988   *Solo Exhibition,* Auburn University Art Gallery, Auburn, Alabama
       Solo Exhibition, Galerie Simonne Stern, Atlanta, Georgia
       Solo Exhibition, Atlanta Fulton Library Gallery, Atlanta, Georgia
       Looking South: A Different Dixie, Birmingham Museum of Art,
         Birmingham, Alabama (traveled)
       Southern Expressions: A Sense of Self, High Museum of Art, Atlanta, Georgia
       State of the Arts: Georgia, Contemporary Arts Center, New Orleans, Louisiana
       Contemporary Georgia Artists/Selections from the Collection, High Museum of
         Art, Atlanta, Georgia

selected honors, awards, grants

1990   *Fellowship Recipient,* Southern Arts Federation/NEA, Atlanta, Georgia
1988   *Individual Artist Grant,* Georgia Council for the Arts, Atlanta, Georgia
       Individual Artist Grant, Fulton County Art Council, Atlanta, Georgia

Biographical Landscape #10, 92.18, 1992, oil on canvas

Sarge, 1993, mixed media on canvas

Virginia Levie

lives in Brooklyn, New York
born 1955 in Huntsville, Alabama
1980 BFA San Francisco Art Institute,
  San Francisco, California
1987-1989 New York Studio School,
  New York, New York

selected recent exhibitions

1994 *Re-inventing the Emblem,* Yale University Art Gallery, New Haven, Connecticut
  Trophies from the Civil / (Wars), The Trophy Room, Memorial Arch, Grand Army
    Plaza, Prospect Park Alliance, Brooklyn, New York
  Small Works, 80 Washington Square East Gallery, New York, New York
1993 *Solo Exhibition, Head First,* Black and White Gallery Marymount Manhattan
    College, New York, New York
  Nature Mort, Eighth Street Gallery, New York, New York
1992 *National Drawing '92,* Trenton State College, Trenton, New Jersey
1991 *One Plus Two,* Bowery Gallery, New York, New York
1990 *NYSS Alumni Show,* Eighth Street Gallery, New York, New York
1988 *Chautauqua Summer Show,* Chautauqua School for the Arts, Chautauqua, New York
1987 *Seldom Seen Figures,* Gallier Hall Gallery, New Orleans Arts Council,
    New Orleans, Louisiana
1986 *SECCA Small Works Invitational,* Southeastern Center for Contemporary Art,
    Winston-Salem, North Carolina
  Artists' Choice, Galerie Simonne Stern, New Orleans, Louisiana
  Introductions '86, Contemporary Arts Center, New Orleans, Louisiana
1985 *Louisiana Competition 1985,* Louisiana Arts and Sciences Center,
    Baton Rouge, Louisiana

Rick Lowe

lives in Houston, Texas
born 1961 in Eufaula, Alabama
1979-1982 Columbus College,
   Columbus, Georgia
1992-1993 Artist-in-Residence,
   Springer Art Center,
   Biloxi, Mississippi

selected recent exhibitions

1994 *Group Exhibition,* Soulstice, Houston, Texas
1993 *Contemporary Identities,* Phoenix Art Museum, Phoenix, Arizona
1992 *Counter Colon-ialismo,* Diverse Works Artspace, Houston, Texas
   (traveled)
   Southwestern Mythology as America, Snug Harbor Cultural Center,
   Staten Island, New York
1991 *Newcomers and Forerunners,* Lamar University, Beaumont, Texas
   Group Exhibition, The Peoples Arts Store, Galveston, Texas
1990 *Solo Exhibition,* Pedazos Del Mundo, Houston, Texas
   Solo Exhibition, Kumba House/Midtown Art Center, Houston, Texas
   The Blues Aesthetic, Blaffer Gallery, University of Houston,
   Houston, Texas
   Messages from the South, Sewell Gallery, Rice University,
   Houston, Texas
1988 *The Texas Triennial,* Contemporary Arts Museum, Houston, Texas
   Houston Area Show, Blaffer Gallery, University of Houston,
   Houston, Texas
   Comment, Nexus Contemporary Arts Center, Atlanta, Georgia

selected honors, awards, grants

1994 *Founding Director,* Project Row Houses, Houston, Texas
   Commissioner, Municipal Arts Commission, City of Houston, Texas
   Peer Review Panelist, Visual Arts, Texas Commission on the Arts
   Austin, Texas (also 1993)
   Executive Board, Diverse Works Artspace, Houston, Texas (also 1993)
   Executive Board, National Association of Artists Organizations,
   Washington, D.C.
   Member, Minority Affairs Committee, Cultural Arts Council of
   Houston, Houston, Texas
1993 *Juror,* Dozier Foundation Grant, Dallas Museum of Art, Dallas, Texas
1992 *Member,* Houston/Harris County Arts Task Force, Artists Committee
   (also 1991), Houston, Texas
   Executive Board, S.C.R.A. P. (Salvageable, Consumerable, Recyclable
   Arts Parts), Houston, Texas (also 1991)
1990 *Co-Founder,* Union of Independent Artists (an artists advocacy group),
   Houston, Texas

Untitled-Triptych, 1994, mixed media

Tierney LaRon Malone

lives in Houston, Texas
born 1964 in Los Angeles, California;
   resided Mobile, Alabama 1971-1982
1982-1986 Texas Southern University,
   Houston, Texas

selected recent exhibitions

1994 *Group Exhibition,* Project Row Houses, Houston, Texas
     Project Row Houses-Project Artists, Robert McClain & Co., Houston, Texas
1993 *Texas Dialogues,* Blue Star Art Space, San Antonio, Texas
     Visual Dialects, Harris Gallery, Houston, Texas
     I Remember The March on Washington Thirty Year Anniversary: 1963-1993,
       Corcoran Gallery of Art, Washington, D.C.
     Introductions, Barnes-Blackman Gallery, Houston, Texas
1992 *Fresh Visions/New Voices,* The Glassell School of Art, The Museum of Fine Arts,
       Houston, Texas (traveled)
     Forerunners and Newcomers Revisited, Lamar University, Beaumont, Texas
     Anti-Trust, Diverse Works Artspace, Houston, Texas
     The Case for Art, Lawndale Art Center/Houston Public Library, Houston, Texas
1991 *Art+Soul=Jazz,* Barnes-Blackman Gallery, Houston, Texas
1990 *Meeting of Two: Statements,* Commerce Street Artist Warehouse, Houston, Texas
     Opening Exhibition, Barnes-Blackman Gallery, Houston, Texas
     Dimensions of African-American Art, University of Houston, Houston, Texas

selected honors, awards, grants

1994 *Individual Grant,* CACH Visual Artist, Cultural Arts Council of Houston, Houston, Texas
     Individual Grant, Kimbrough Visual Artist Grant, Dallas Museum of Art, Dallas, Texas

Ed McGowin

lives in New York, New York
born 1938 in Hattiesburg, Mississippi
1961 BS University of Southern Mississippi,
  Hattiesburg, Mississippi
1964 MFA University of Alabama, Tuscaloosa,
  Alabama

selected recent exhibitions

1994 *Ed McGowin Narrative Sculpture,* The Paris-New York-Bangkok Gallery,
  Bangkok, Thailand
  Ed McGowin: Sculpture, Anderson Gallery, Buffalo, New York
  Thirty Something: A 30th Anniversary Celebration, Fine Arts Museum of
    the South, Mobile, Alabama
  The Joker is Wild, Blondies Fine Art, New York, New York
1993 *Solo Exhibition,* Paris-New York-Kent Gallery, Kent, Connecticut
  X Sightings 93, Anderson Gallery, Buffalo, New York
  In the Ring, Snug Harbor Cultural Center, Staten Island, New York
  The Bridge Sings the Blues, Bridge Center for Contemporary Art, El Paso, Texas
  Pets: Artists and An American Obsession, The Charles A. Wustum Museum of
    Fine Arts, Racine, Wisconsin
  Foundation 'Oxygen' International Biennial, Gyor, Hungary
  Books, Barbara Gillman Gallery, Miami, Florida
  Oro D'Autore, Arezzo, Italy
1992 *Solo Exhibition,* Jones Troyer Fitzpatrick Gallery, Washington, D.C.
  The Book as Art, 1960 to Now, The Heckscher Museum, Huntington, New York
  Artists Known and New, Paris-New York-Kent Gallery, Kent, Connecticut
  Beyond Realism: Image and Enigma in American Art, Southern Alleghenies
    Museum, Loretto, Pennsylvania
  Dogs, Levison Kane Gallery, Boston, Massachusetts
1991 *Ed McGowin, Paintings,* Boca Raton Museum of Art, Boca Raton, Florida
  Ed McGowin, Hokin Kaufman Inc., Chicago, Illinois
  Ed McGowin, Margulies Talpin Gallery, Miami, Florida
  Too Wit: Timely Objects with Ironic Tendencies, Rosa Esman Gallery,
    New York, New York
  Large Scale Drawings, Middendorf Gallery, Washington, D.C.
  The Eternal Male, Sherry French Gallery, New York

selected honors, awards, grants

1994 *Commission for Sculpture,* Dallas Rapid Transit Authority, Dallas, Texas
1993 *Commission for Sculpture,* City of Jubail, Saudi Arabia, The Royal Commission,
    Kingdom of Saudi Arabia
1992 *Mural Commission,* Occupational Rehabilitation Center, Coney Island, New York,
    Percent for Art Sculpture Commission, Department of Cultural Affairs, New York
1991 *Travel Grant for "Outsider Art," Malmo, Sweden,* S.U.N.Y., New York
1990 *Individual Recognition,* Hattiesburg Arts Council, Hattiesburg, Mississippi

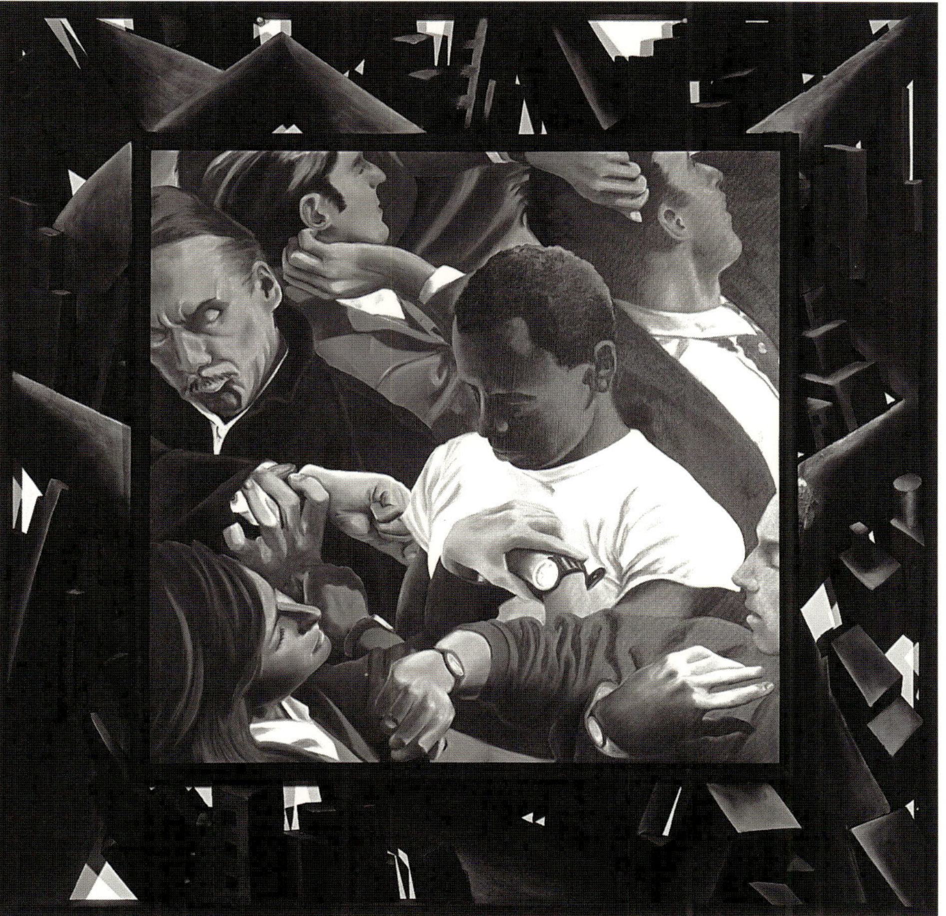

Metropolitan Adults, 1991, oil on canvas with painted wood frame

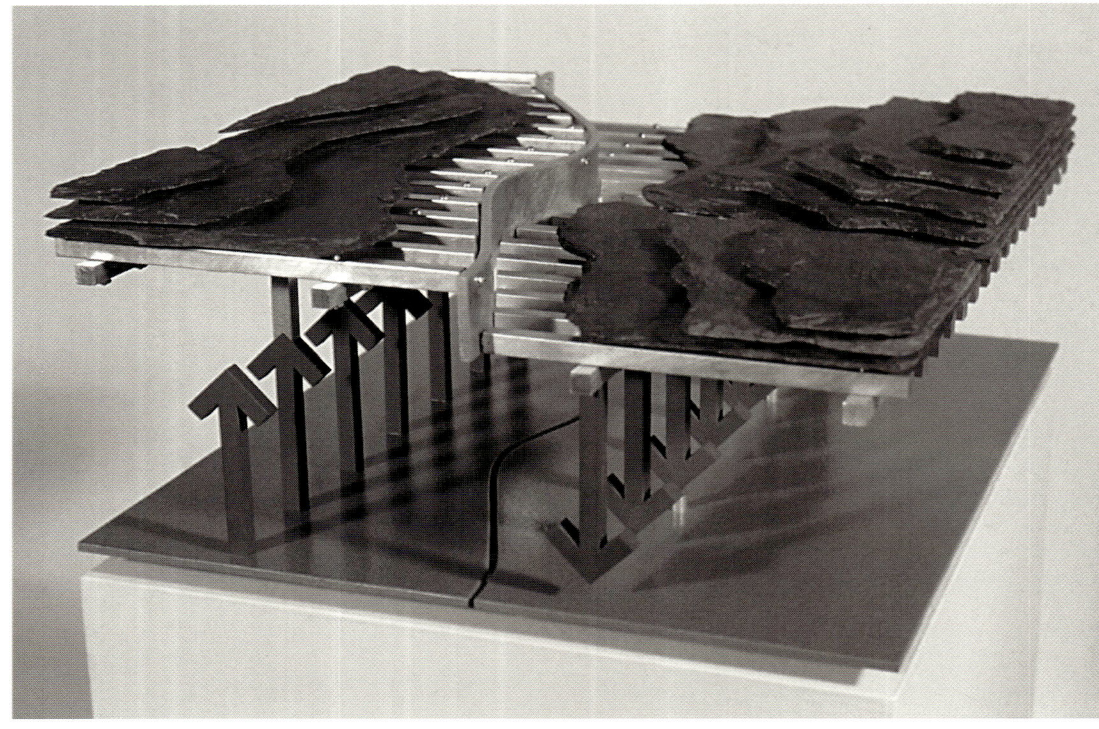

Faultzone, 1986, aluminum, slate & painted steel

Ted Metz

lives in Montevallo, Alabama
born 1949 in Columbus, Ohio
1971 BFA Old Dominion University,
 Norfolk, Virginia
1973 University of South Carolina,
 Columbia, South Carolina

selected recent exhibitions

1994 *Metz and Stephens,* Birmingham Southern College,
 Birmingham, Alabama

1991 *Metz, Meyer, Stephens Exhibition,* Troy State University,
 Troy, Alabama

1989 *City on a Hill: Twenty Years of Artists at Cortona,* Georgia
 Museum of Art, Athens, Georgia (traveled)
 Birmingham Artists 1959-1989, Birmingham Museum of Art,
 Birmingham, Alabama

1988 *La Grange National VIII,* Chattahoochee Valley Art Museum
 and Lamar Dodd Art Center, La Grange College,
 LaGrange, Georgia
 Annual Bi-State Art Competition, Meridian Museum of Art,
 Meridian, Mississippi
 Out of the Closet-Atypical Works, BAA Gallery, Birmingham
 Museum of Art, Birmingham, Alabama
 Reunion Exhibition (Cortona Faculty/Artist in Residence),
 Georgia Museum of Art, Athens, Georgia

1987 *Whirlpool Foundation National Sculpture Exhibition,* Krasl
 Art Center, St. Joseph, Michigan (traveled)
 The Southeastern Juried Exhibition, Fine Arts Museum of the
 South, Mobile, Alabama
 Faculty Exhibition, University of Montevallo, Montevallo,
 Alabama
 Faculty Exhibition, University of Georgia Studies Abroad
 Program, Palazzo Casali, Cortona, Italy
 Visual Artists Fellowship Exhibition, Alabama State Council
 on the Arts Gallery, Montgomery, Alabama

selected honors, awards, grants

1989 *Regional Fellowship in Sculpture Finalist,* Southern Arts
 Federationa/NEA, Atlanta, Georgia

1987 *Nomination,* Awards in the Visual Arts, National
 Endowment for the Arts, Washington, D.C. (and 1982)

1986 *Individual Artist Fellowship Grant,* Alabama State Council
 on the Arts, Montgomery, Alabama

Lanford Monroe

lives in Taos, New Mexico
born 1950 in Bridgeport, Connecticut;
    resided Huntsville, Alabama
    1964-1972, 1978-1991
1968 Birmingham Southern College,
    Birmingham, Alabama
1969-1971 Ringling School of Art,
    Sarasota, Florida

selected recent exhibitions

1994 *Lanford Monroe/John Ruthven,* Trailside-Americana Galleries,
    Jackson, Wyoming
National Academy of Western Art, National Cowboy Hall of Fame,
    Oklahoma City, Oklahoma
American Women Artists and the West, Tucson Museum of Art,
    Tucson, Arizona (also 1993)
Western Visions, National Wildlife Art Museum (formerly Wildlife
    of the American West Art Museum), Jackson, Wyoming
Art for the Parks Competition, Top 100, National Park Academy
    of the Arts, Jackson, Wyoming (also 1991)
1993 *American Art in Miniature,* Gilcrease Museum, Tulsa, Oklahoma
Wildlife-The Artist's View, Leigh Yawkey Woodson Art Museum,
    Wausau, Wisconsin
Natural Wonders, Leigh Yawkey Woodson Art Museum,
    Wausau, Wisconsin
1992 *National Academy of Western Art (Guest Artist),* National Cowboy
    Hall of Fame, Oklahoma City, Oklahoma
American Academy of Equine Art, National Museum of the Horse,
    Lexington, Kentucky (also 1990)
1991 *Encounters 17: Lanford Monroe,* Huntsville Museum of Art,
    Huntsville, Alabama
1990 *Western Visions,* Wildlife of the American West Art Museum,
    Jackson, Wyoming
Miniatures '90, White Oak Gallery, Edina, Minnesota
Society of Animal Artists 30th Annual Exhibition, St. Hubert's
    Giralda, Madison, New Jersey

selected honors, awards, grants

1994 *Judges Award and Grand Teton National Parks Award,* Art for the
    Parks Competition, Top 100, National Park Academy of the Arts,
    Jackson, Wyoming
Special Exhibition, Honored Along with Parents, Huntsville
    Museum of Art, Huntsville, Alabama
1991 *U. S. Art Magazine Award,* Arts for the Parks Competition Top 100

Sunday Morning, 1990, oil on panel

Elegy Suite #7, 1994, oil, graphite & tempera on paper

Deborah Muirhead

lives in Storrs, Conncticut
born 1949 in Bessemer, Alabama
1973 BFA Illinois Wesleyan University, Bloomington, Illinois
1975 MS Illinois State University, Normal, Illinois
1980 MFA Illinois State University, Normal, Illinois

selected recent exhibitions

1994 *Southern Roots-Women's Voices,* Dalton Gallery, Agnes Scott College, Decatur, Georgia
New American Talent: Tenth Exhibition, Laguna Gloria Art Museum, Austin, Texas
1993 *Solo Exhibition,* Fitchburg State College, Fitchburg, Massachusetts
Affinities-Recent Work, The Gallery of Contemporary Art, Sacred Heart University, Fairfield, Connecticut
American Drawing Biennial IV, Muscarelle Museum of Art, College of William and Mary, Williamsburg, Virginia
1992 *Solo Exhibition,* Widner Gallery, Trinity College, Hartford, Connecticut
Present Tense, UWM Fine Arts Gallery, University of Wisconsin-Milwaukee, Milwaukee, Wisconsin
Gifted Visions: African American Artists, Lyman Allyn Art Museum, New London, Connecticut
Resonance, Lyman Allyn Art Museum, New London, Connecticut
1991 *Solo Exhibition,* Illinois State University, Normal, Illinois
Solo Exhibition, New Space Gallery, Manchester, Connecticut
9 Artists/9 Visions: 1991, DeCordova Museum, Lincoln, Massachusetts
Second Connecticut Biennial, Bruce Museum, Greenwich, Connecticut
Greater Midwest International Award Winners Exhibition, Central Missouri State University, Warrensburg, Missouri
42nd Annual Art of the Northeast USA, Silvermine Gallery, New Canaan, Connecticut
1990 *Spirit Calls,* Artworks Gallery, Hartford, Connecticut
New Works, Connecticut Gallery, Marbourgh, Connecticut
Greater International Exhibit, Central Missouri State University, Warrensburg, Missouri
1989 *Solo Exhibition,* Promenade Gallery, Hartford, Connecticut
Embracing Mystery, Souyun Yi Gallery, New York, New York
Spirit in the Paint/Spirit in the Wood, Artspace Gallery, New Haven, Connecticut
Natural Image, Stamford Museum, Stamford, Connecticut

selected honors, awards, grants

1994 *Juror's Merit Award,* "New American Talent: Tenth Exhibition," Laguna Gloria Art Museum, Austin, Texas
1991 *Individual Artist Grant,* Connecticut Commission on the Arts, Hartford, Connecticut
1990 *Exhibition Award,* Greater Midwest International Exhibition, Central Missouri State University, Warrensburg, Missouri
Faculty Research Grant, University of Connecticut, Storrs, Connecticut
1988 *Visiting Faculty Fellow,* Yale University, New Haven, Connecticut (also 1987)

Pat Mulherin

lives in Decatur, Georgia
born 1956 in Mobile, Alabama
1978 Atlanta College of Art,
   Atlanta, Georgia
1980 BFA Georgia State University,
   Atlanta, Georgia
1985 Texas Tech University,
   Lubbock, Texas

selected recent exhibitions

1993 *Photographs from the Great Flood of 1993,* Emory University, Atlanta, Georgia
   Group Exhibition, The Green Room, Northlake Tower Festival, Atlanta, Georgia
   Gala Opening Exhibition, The Perrin Center for the Arts, Roswell, Georgia
   Faculty Exhibit, DeKalb College, Atlanta, Georgia (also 1992 and 1991)
   ArtCare AIDS Benefit Show, Swissotel, Atlanta, Georgia
1992 *Best of the Best,* Colony Square, Atlanta, Georgia
   The Wild West Show, Exhibit A Gallery, Atlanta, Georgia
   ArtCare Aids Benefit Show, Hotel Nikko, Atlanta, Georgia
1991 *The Photography Show,* Exhibit A Gallery, Atlanta, Georgia
1990 *Solo Exhibition,* Emory University at Oxford, Oxford, Georgia
1989 *Images and Visions,* DeKalb College, Atlanta, Georgia

Janet Nolan

lives in New York, New York
born 1942 in Montgomery, Alabama
1964 BFA Auburn University,
  Auburn, Alabama
1976 MFA Georgia State University,
  Atlanta, Georgia

selected recent exhibitions

1994 *Personal Property,* Art in General, New York, New York
  Contemporary Women Artists, Hackley School Gallery,
    Westchester, New York
  Spider's Parlor, Studio Installation, New York, New York
  Terrible Beauty, Dru Arstark Gallery, New York, New York
  Whateva, Dru Arstark Gallery, New York, New York
1991 *Ocean Earth,* American Fine Art Gallery, New York, New York
1990 *In The Round,* Mary Delahoyd Gallery, New York, New York
  Pro Found, Outer Space Gallery, New York, New York
  Painted Metal, City Without Walls Gallery, Newark, New Jersey
1989 *Solo Exhibition, Wings and Armor,* Fayerweather Gallery,
    University of Virginia, Charlottesville, Virginia
  Catfish and Honeybee (Stage Set), Aerodance Group,
    New York, New York
  Show Your Metal, Selena Gallery, Long Island University,
    Brooklyn, New York
1988 *Holiday Invitational,* Soho 20, New York, New York
  Small Works Invitational, Bowery Gallery, New York, New York

Matt Nolen

lives in New York, New York
born 1960 in Key West, Florida
1969-1975 Gadsden Museum School, Gadsden
  Museum of Art, Gadsden, Alabama
1982 Studies Abroad Program, School of
  Architecture, Auburn University,
  Auburn, Alabama
1983 BA Auburn University, Auburn, Alabama

selected recent exhibitions

1994 *Solo Exhibition,* Everson Museum of Art, Syracuse, New York
  Solo Exhibition, Garth Clark Gallery, Los Angeles, California
  Extravagant Teapots, Nancy Margolis Gallery, New York, New York
1993 *Solo Exhibition, The Apothecary Series,* ARCHON, New York, New York
  Solo Exhibition, Time Ladders, Artspace, John Michael Kohler Arts Center,
    Sheboygan, Wisconsin
  29th Ceramic National Exhibition, Jurors, Rudy Autio, Robert Ellison, Jr.,
    Ronald A. Kuchta, Martha Drexler Lynn, Everson Museum of Art, Syracuse,
    New York (traveled)
  Soup Tureens: 1993, Helen Drutt Gallery, Philadelphia, Pennsylvania
  Sex Money Politics, Nancy Drysdale Gallery, Washington, D.C.
  Clay 1993: A National Survey, William Traver Gallery, Seattle, Washington
  Subversive Crafts, MIT List Visual Arts Center, Massachusetts Institute of
    Technology, Cambridge, Massachusetts
  Titanic Tea, Garth Clark Gallery, New York, New York
  The Framed Teapot, PRO-ART, St. Louis, Missouri
1992 *Charles Crowley/Matt Nolen,* Kavesh Gallery, Ketchum, Idaho
  Emerging Talent, Juried, NCECA, Philadelphia, Pennsylvania
  7th Annual San Angelo National Ceramic Competition, Juror, Wayne Higby,
    San Angelo, Texas (traveled)
  The Clay Cup, Juror, Ron Nagle, Abington Art Center, Jenkinstown,
    Pennsylvania
  A show about the cup, ARCHON, New York, New York
  The Candelabra, PRO-ART, St. Louis, Missouri
1991 *Solo Exhibition,* ARCHON, New York, New York (also 1989)
  47th International Ceramic Art Competition, Palazzo delle Exposizioni,
    Faenza, Italy
  Ceramics Now, Juried, Downey Museum of Art, Downey, California
  The Wichita National, Juror, Marcia Manhart, The Wichita Center for the Arts,
    Wichita, Kansas
  Personal Shrines and Icons, Jurors, Syd Carpenter, Robert Pfannebacker, David
    Wright, The Clay Studio, Philadelphia, Pennsylvania
  Rituals of Tea, Garth Clark Gallery, New York
1990 *Group Exhibition,* ARCHON, New York

selected honors, awards, grants

1994 Statewide Artist Workshop Program, The Virginia Museum of Fine Arts,
    Richmond, Virginia (thru 1996)
1991 *Grant Recipient,* Empire State Crafts Alliance, Syracuse, New York

Wedding Urn, 1994, glazed porcelain

Celery Chair with Peppers, Carrots & Snow Pea, 1993, swiss pear and leather

Craig Nutt

lives in Northport, Alabama
born 1950 in Belmond, Iowa
1972 BA University of Alabama,
Tuscaloosa, Alabama

selected recent exhibitions

1994 *Craig Nutt and Sarah Rakes,* Blue Spiral Gallery, Asheville,
North Carolina
The Fifth International Shoebox Exhibition, University of Hawaii,
Honolulu, Hawaii (traveled)
Wood Invitational, Alabama A & M University, Normal, Alabama
Craig Nutt: Flying Vegetables, The Art of the Toy, Scottsdale, Arizona
Pull Up a Chair 3, Meredith Gallery, Baltimore, Maryland
Whirligigs and Weathervanes: Contemporary Sculpture, Visual Arts
Resources, Eugene, Oregon (traveled)
1993 *Solo Exhibition,* Meredith Gallery, Baltimore, Maryland
Contemporary Crafts: The National Scene, Kentucky Art and Craft
Council, Louisville, Kentucky
Year of Craft Showcase, Alabama State Council on the Arts Gallery,
Montgomery, Alabama
Alabama Contemporary Crafts, Wiregrass Museum of Art, Dothan,
Alabama
One of A Kind: Contemporary Furniture from the Southeast, Atlanta
International Museum, Atlanta, Georgia
*The Furniture Show: Contemporary Interpretations in Wood and
Mixed Media,* Show of Hands, Denver, Colorado
1992 *Artists, Architects and Designers: Furniture of Our Century,* High
Museum of Art at Georgia Pacific, Atlanta, Georgia
Seeds of Change, National Museum of Natural History, Smithsonian
Institution, Washington, D.C.
Feet First: The Shoe Show, (with Gaza Bowen), Sarratt Gallery,
Vanderbilt University, Nashville, Tennessee
Revolving Techniques, James A. Michener Museum, Doylestown,
Pennsylvania
Lathe-Turned Objects Defined III: Functional and Sculptural,
The Society of Arts and Crafts, Boston, Massachusetts
Kinetic Art, The Gallery at Studio B, Lancaster, Ohio
Serious Fun, Society of Contemporary Crafts, Pittsburgh, Pennsylvania
Contentious Crafts, Nexus Contemporary Art Center, Atlanta, Georgia
Wood in Disguise, Southern Ohio Museum, Portsmouth, Ohio
1991 *Artists and the American Yard,* Charles A. Wustum Museum of Fine
Arts, Racine, Wisconsin
Crafted Environments, The Southern Arts Federation/NEA Awards in
Crafts, Galleria 300, Atlanta, Georgia
International Lathe-Turned Objects; Challenge IV, Port of History
Museum, Philadelphia, Pennsylvania

selected honors, awards, grants

1990 *Druid Arts Award,* Tuscaloosa, Alabama Arts Council
1989 *Fellowship Recipient,* Southern Arts Federation/NEA, Atlanta, Georgia
1988 *Individual Artist Fellowship Grant,* Alabama State Council on the Arts
Harriet Murray Memorial Award, Birmingham Museum of Art,
Birmingham, Alabama

Happy Birthday Baby!, 1994, oil on canvas (not included in the exhibition)

David Parrish

lives in Huntsville, Alabama
born 1939 in Birmingham, Alabama
1957-1958 Washington and Lee University,
   Lexington, Virginia
1961 BFA University of Alabama,
   Tuscaloosa, Alabama

selected recent exhibitions

1994 *Elvis + Marilyn, 2 x Immortal,* Institute of Contemporary Art,
   Boston, Massachusetts (traveled)
   Solo Exhibition, Louis K. Meisel Gallery, New York (also 1992 and 1990)
1993 *American Realism: The Urban Scene (Selections from the Glenn C. Janss
   Collection),* Boise Art Museum, Boise, Idaho *(traveled)*
   Photorealism Since 1980, Louis K. Meisel Gallery, New York, New York
   Really Real, Realism Show, Jack Wright Gallery, Palm Beach, Florida
1992 *Some Faces,* Louis K. Meisel Gallery, New York, New York
   Photorealism from Nashville Collections, Cheekwood Fine Arts Center,
   Nashville, Tennessee
1991 *Photo-Realism: Revisited,* Museum of Art, Fort Lauderdale, Florida
1990 *Amerikansk Fotorealism,* Art Now Gallery, Göteborg, Sweden

Ring Round Rosie, 1993, oil on canvas

Dennis Potter

lives in San Francisco, California
born 1950 in Oak Ridge, Tennessee;
resided Huntsville, Alabama
1963-1978
1973 BA University of Alabama in
Huntsville, Huntsville, Alabama
1978-79 San Francisco Art Institute,
San Francisco, California
1981 MA University of California,
Berkeley, Berkeley, California
1983 MFA University of California,
Berkeley, Berkeley, California

selected recent exhibitions

1993 *Artist-in-Residence,* Kala Institute, Berkeley, California
Gallery Member's Summer Show, Germans Van Eck Gallery,
New York, New York (also 1992 and 1991)
Gallery Member's Summer Show, Stephen Wirtz Gallery,
San Francisco, California (also 1991)

1992 *Apocalypse and Rebirth,* The Gallery Three Zero, New York, New York
Solo Exhibition, Germans Van Eck Gallery, New York, New York

1991 *Solo Exhibition,* Stephen Wirtz Gallery, San Francisco, California

1989 *Group Exhibition,* Fort Mason Rental Gallery, Museum of Modern Art,
San Francisco, California

1988 *Annual Juried Competition,* Berkeley Art Center, Walnut Street,
Berkeley, California

1987 *In Memoriam,* Donald Lawson Gallery, San Francisco, California
Annual Juried Competition, Berkeley Art Center, Walnut Street,
Berkeley, California

selected honors, awards, grants

1994 *Fellow,* Macdowell Colony, Peterborough, New Hampshire

1988 *Juror's Award,* "Annual Juried Competition," Berkeley Art Center,
Walnut Street, Berkeley, California (also 1987)

Stephen Rolfe Powell

lives in Danville, Kentucky
born 1951 in Birmingham, Alabama
1974 BA Centre College, Danville, Kentucky
1980 Alabama Teaching Certificate,
   Birmingham-Southern College,
   Birmingham, Alabama
1983 MFA Louisiana State University,
   Baton Rouge, Louisiana

selected recent exhibitions

1994 *Solo Exhibition,* Marx Gallery, Chicago, Illinois
   Solo Exhibition, Galerie L, Hamburg, Germany
   Solo Exhibition, Habatat Gallery, Aspen, Colorado
   Solo Exhibition, Bell Gallery, Memphis, Tennessee
   Thirty Something: A 30th Anniversary Celebration, Fine Arts Museum of the South,
      Mobile, Alabama
   Contemporary Art Cincinnati, Contemporary Arts Center, Cincinnati, Ohio
   Glass Invitational, Hodgell Gallery, Sarasota, Florida
   Contemporary Glass Invitational, Concept Art Gallery, Pittsburgh, Pennsylvania
   Glass America 1994, Heller Gallery, New York (also 1993, 1992, and 1991)
   Transitions '94, Paramont Art Center, Ashland, Kentucky (traveled)
   International Invitational, Habatat Galleries, Farmington Hills, Michigan
      (also 1993, 1992, and 1991)
   Centre Glass, Elizabethtown Community College, Elizabethtown, Kentucky
1993 *Solo Exhibition,* Habatat Galleries, Farmington Hills, Michigan (also 1991)
   Solo Exhibition, Marta Hewett Gallery, Cincinnati, Ohio
   Solo Exhibition, Kentucky Art and Craft Foundation, Louisville, Kentucky
   Harmony in Glass, Marx Gallery, Chicago, Illinois
   Contemporary Glass, Museum of Art, Fort Lauderdale, Florida
   Leight Collection, J.B. Speed Art Museum, Louisville, Kentucky
   Contemporary Traditions, The Kentucky Museum, Bowling Green, Kentucky
1992 *Solo Exhibition,* Habatat Gallery, Boca Raton, Florida (also 1991)
   Solo Exhibition, Kimzey Miller Gallery, Seattle, Washington (also 1990)
   Solo Exhibition, Harris Gallery, Houston, Texas
   Solo Exhibition, Kirvan Bartoszewicz Gallery, Palm Springs, California
      (also 1991 and 1990)
   Cristalomancia, Rufino Tamayo Museum, Mexico City, Mexico (traveled to
      Museo de Arte Contemporáneo, Monterrey, Mexico)
   Europ'Art, Genève-Palexpo, Genève, Switzerland
   200 Years of Kentucky Craft, Owensboro Museum and the Kentucky Art and
      Craft Foundation, Louisville, Kentucky
1990 *Solo Exhibition,* Sarah Squeri Gallery, Cincinnati, Ohio
   Contemporary Glass, Contemporary Crafts Gallery, Portland, Oregon
   Centre Glass, The Parthenon, Centennial Park, Nashville, Tennessee

selected honors, awards, grants

1992 *Harriet Murray Memorial Award,* Birmingham Museum of Art, Birmingham, Alabama

Addiction Cleavage Johnson, 1993, blown glass

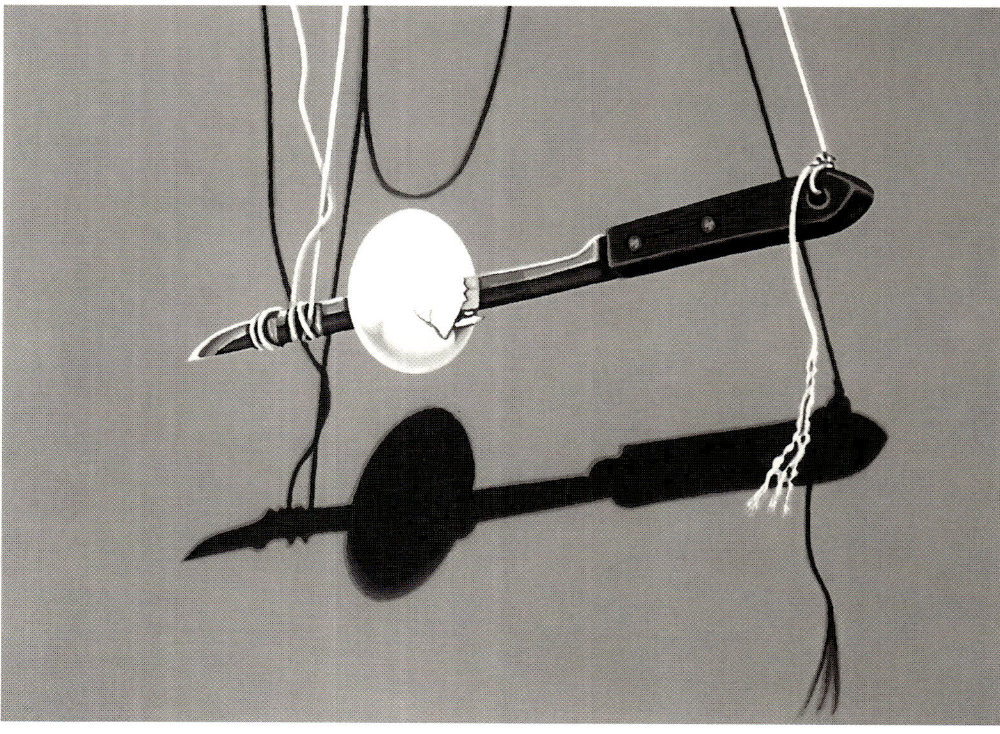

Egg Series VI: Knife, 1988, screen serigraph on paper

Joe Price

lives in Sonora, California
born 1935 in Ferriday, Louisiana;
   resided Decatur, Alabama 1945-1957
1957 BS Northwestern University,
   Evanston, Illinois
1967-1968 Art Center College of Design,
   Los Angeles, California
1970 MA Stanford University, Palo Alto, California

selected recent exhibitions

1991 *International Print Triennale '91,* Krakow, Poland
     Audubon Artists 49th Annual Exhibition, New York, New York
     1991 National Printmaking Exhibition, Juror, Richard Haas, Trenton
       State College, Trenton, New Jersey
     15th Annual National Drawing Exhibition, N.R. Eppink Gallery,
       Emporia State University, Emporia, Kansas
1990 *Solo Exhibition,* Coastal Arts League Museum of Art, Half Moon Bay,
       California
     Solo Exhibition, Wenniger Graphics, Boston, Massachusetts
       (also 1989 and 1988)
     Interprint, Lviv, U.S.S.R.
     Breaking New Ground, Peninsula Art Association, San Mateo, California
     Notable Detail: Six American Contemporary Printmakers, Haggar
       University Gallery, University of Dallas, Dallas, Texas
     With Nothing On: Prints and Drawings by American Artists,
       New Orleans Museum of Art, New Orleans, Louisiana
     Pacific Prints 5th Biennial Print Competition, Palo Alto, California
1989 *New Works: A Group Show,* Ankrum Gallery, Los Angeles, California
     Cimarron National Works on Paper, Oklahoma State University,
       Stillwater, Oklahoma
     Audubon Artists 47th Annual Exhibition, New York, New York
     5th International Biennale Petit Format de Papier, Musée du Petit
       Format, Couvin, Belgium
     15th International Independante Exhibition of Prints, Kanagawa,
       Yokahama, Japan (also 1987, 1986, 1985, 1984, and 1983)
     Courier for the Interchange of Small Stampe, 3rd Biennial,
       Havana, Cuba
     The 4th International Biennial Print Exhibit, Taipei Fine Arts Museum,
       Taipei, Taiwan, Republic of China

selected honors, awards, grants

1991 *Silver Medal,* "Audubon Artists 49th Annual Exhibition,"
     New York, New York
1990 *Pacific Art League Serigraphy Award,* "Pacific Prints 5th Biennial Print
     Competition," Palo Alto, California
1989 *First Creative Achievement Award,* California State Legislature/Arts
     Council of San Mateo County, California
1988 *Moses Lasky Award for Serigraphy,* "4th Biennial Print Competition,"
     Palo Alto, California

Jim Richard

lives in New Orleans, Louisiana
born 1943 in Port Arthur, Texas
1965 BS Lamar State University,
    Beaumont, Texas
1968 MFA University of Colorado,
    Boulder, Colorado
Taught Spring Hill College,
    Mobile, Alabama 1968-1972

selected recent exhibitions

1993 *Inaugural Exhibition,* Morris Museum of Art, Augusta, Georgia
15th Anniversary Exhibition, Arthur Roger Gallery, New Orleans, Louisiana
1992 *Gallery Artists,* Arthur Roger Gallery, New Orleans, Louisiana
1991 *Just What Is It That Makes Today's Homes So Different, So Appealing,* Hyde
    Collection, Glens Falls, New York
Visionary Imagism, Contemporary Arts Center, New Orleans, Louisiana
1990 *Art of the Seventies and Eighties,* New Orleans Museum of Art,
    New Orleans, Louisiana
1989 *Fifty Master Drawings from the New Orleans Museum of Art,* New Orleans
    Museum of Art, New Orleans, Louisiana (traveled)
Personal Visions, The Watson Gallery, Houston, Texas
1988 *The Drawing Show: Artists Who Have Exhibited at the Drawing Center in
    New York,* Massachusetts College of Art, Boston, Massachusetts
Ten Year Anniversary Exhibition, Arthur Roger Gallery,
    New Orleans, Louisiana
Artists from New Orleans, Barbara Gillman Gallery, Miami, Florida
1987 *10 Years of Southeast Seven,* Southeastern Center for Contemporary Art,
    Winston-Salem, North Carolina
Group Exhibition, New Orleans Museum of Art, New Orleans, Louisiana
Ten Ways of Looking at Landscapes, The Watson Gallery, Houston, Texas
Group Exhibition, Arthur Roger Gallery, New Orleans, Louisiana

Owning Modern Sculpture, 1993, mixed media on paper

Night Puddle, 1989, cibachrome

Sonja Rieger

lives in Birmingham, Alabama
born 1953 in Ansbach, Germany
1976 BA The University of
    Massachusetts,
    Amherst, Massachusetts
1979 MFA Rutgers University,
    New Brunswick, New Jersey

selected recent exhibitions

1994 *Birmingham: Into the Night,* Blue Spiral Gallery, Asheville,
    North Carolina
    The Rena Self Collection, The Birmingham Museum of Art,
    Birmingham, Alabama
1992 *ESP: Emerging Southern Photographers,* Memphis College of
    Art, Memphis, Tennessee
    *The Birmingham Airport Authority, Commission for Airport
    Renovation,* Permanent Installation, Birmingham, Alabama
    Hot Water, Faculty Exhibition, 10-2-4 Gallery,
    Birmingham, Alabama
1991 *Recollecting the Remembered Landscape,* Jones Troyer
    Fitzpatrick Gallery, Washington, D.C.
    Selections from the Permanent Collection, Birmingham
    Museum of Art, Birmingham, Alabama
    Selections SPE Opening Exhibition, A Gallery of Fine
    Photography, New Orleans, Louisiana
1990 *Current Works,* Juror, Charles Stainbach, Society for
    Contemporary Photography, Kansas City, Missouri
1989 *Birmingham Collects Photography,* The Birmingham
    Museum of Art, Birmingham, Alabama
    In View of Home: Alabama Landscape Photography,
    Huntsville Museum of Art, Huntsville, Alabama (traveled)
    *Birmingham Hitachi Exhibition of Contemporary Birmingham
    Artists,* Hitachi Cultural Center, Hitachi, Japan

selected honors, awards, grants

1990 *Faculty Research Grant, The Investigation of Computer
    Generated Photography,* University of Alabama at Birmingham,
    Birmingham, Alabama
1989 *Media/Photography Grant,* Alabama State Council on the Arts,
    Montgomery, Alabama

Mary Ann Sampson

lives in Ragland, Alabama
born 1941 in Smithfield, North Carolina
1963 RN North Carolina Baptist Hospital School
   of Nursing, Winston-Salem, North Carolina
1982 BA Samford University, Birmingham,
   Alabama
1988 and 1991, Penland School, Penland,
   North Carolina

selected recent exhibitions

1993 *Alabama Contemporary Women Artists Exhibition,* Alabama State Council on
   the Arts Gallery, Montgomery, Alabama
   Hands at Work: A Celebration of American Book Crafts, The University of Alabama-
   Book Arts Gallery, Tuscaloosa, Alabama
   Group Exhibition, The Town Meeting Hall, Seaside, Florida
1992 *In/Outsiders from the American South-1992 Montgomery-Biennial,* Montgomery
   Museum of Fine Arts, Montgomery, Alabama
   Visual Songs and Bone Dances, The University of Alabama-Book Arts Gallery,
   Tuscaloosa, Alabama
1991 *War and Peace,* The Center for Book Arts, New York, New York
   Bookworks by Three Alabama Artists, Air University Library, Maxwell Air Force
   Base, Montgomery, Alabama
   Book Arts-Four Approaches, The Birmingham Public Library,
   Birmingham, Alabama
   Installations, Drawings, and Books, The Kennedy-Douglass Center for the Arts,
   Florence, Alabama
   Thirteenth Annual Miniworks on Paper, Jacksonville State University,
   Jacksonville, Alabama (also 1990 and 1989)
1990 *Book Exhibition,* Maralyn Wilson Gallery, Birmingham, Alabama
   Art and the Alabama Woman, Mobile College, Mobile, Alabama
   Drawing Exhibition-Southern Graphics, Birmingham-Southern College,
   Birmingham, Alabama
   The Print Show, Maralyn Wilson Gallery, Birmingham, Alabama
1988 *Peregrinations-Events-Departures,* Space One Eleven, Birmingham, Alabama
   (traveled to Virginia Intermont College, Bristol, Virginia; The Rowe Gallery,
   University of North Carolina at Charlotte; and Georgetown College,
   Georgetown, Kentucky)
   The Red Clay Survey: First Biennial Exhibition of Contemporary Southern Art,
   Huntsville Museum of Art, Huntsville, Alabama

selected honors, awards, grants

1993 *Artist-in-Residence,* The Seaside Institute, Seaside, Florida
1992 *Artists' Board Member,* Space One Eleven, Birmingham, Alabama
   Executive Board, Magic City Art Connection, Birmingham, Alabama (since 1986)
1990 *Executive Board,* Birmingham Art Association, Birmingham, Alabama (since 1985)
1986 *President,* Birmingham Art Association, Birmingham, Alabama

An Opera in My Barn, 1994, mixed media

David Sandlin

lives in New York, New York
born 1956 Belfast, Northern Ireland
1979 BA University of Alabama at
    Birmingham, Birmingham, Alabama

selected recent exhibitions

1993 *Solo Exhibition, Waltz Across Sinland,* Linden Hall, Melbourne, Australia
    Solo Exhibition, Sanitized for Your Pleasure, Sai Gallery, Tokyo, Japan
    Cadavre Exquis, Drawing Center, New York, New York
    Comic Power, "Sin-E-Plex" Installation at Exit Art, New York, New York
    Graf/X, Bess Cutler Gallery, New York, New York
    The Pet Show, Helander Gallery, New York, New York
    Comix Brut, Brody's Gallery, Washington, D.C.
    Visceral Landscapes, Carl Hammer Gallery, Chicago, Illinois

1992 *Solo Exhibition, Burning Ring of Fire,* Haynes Fine Art Gallery, Montana
    State University, Bozeman, Montana (traveled to SMASH Gallery of Modern
      Art, Vancouver, B.C., Canada; Carl Hammer Gallery, Chicago, Illinois; and
      Printed Matter, New York, New York)
    New Images, Carl Hammer Gallery, Chicago, Illinois
    Goodbye to Apple Pie, DeCordova Museum, Lincoln, Massachusetts
    Writing on the Walls, Gallery 303, New York, New York
    Fear of Painting, Arthur Roger Gallery, New York, New York
    New Work, New York, What Gallery, Tokyo, Japan
    Reframing Cartoons, Wexner Art Center for the Arts, The Ohio State
      University, Columbus, Ohio
    Benefit for the Asian Women's Center, Asian Women's Center, New York, New York

1991 *Solo Exhibition, The 7 Seas of Sin,* Gracie Mansion Gallery, New York, New York
    Solo Exhibition, Luv-Motel, Barneys, New York, New York
    Misfit Lit, COCA Center for Contemporary Art, Seattle, Washington (traveled to
      SMASH Gallery for Modern Art, Vancouver, B.C., Canada; L.A.C.E.,
      Los Angeles, California)
    New York Goods, Gallery Itoya, Tokyo, Japan
    The PEP Painting Show, Gallery, Itoya, Tokyo, Japan
    The Raw and the Hard Boiled, Paper Heros Gallery, Melbourne, Australia
    Prix de HOME 1991, HOME, New York, New York
    The Human Condition, Hyde Park Art Center, Hyde Park, Illinois
    Post Pop and Beyond, Bess Cutler Gallery, Santa Monica, California

1990 *Solo Exhibition, Voyage to Sinland,* Carl Hammer Gallery, Chicago, Illinois
    Solo Exhibition, Satin Sheets, Art Awareness Gallery, Lexington, Kentucky
    The Great American Fax Attack, Andrea Ruggieri, Washington, D.C.
    New Work-New York, Helander Gallery, Palm Beach, Florida
    Re: Framing Cartoons, Loughelton Gallery, New York, New York

Robert A. Schaefer, Jr.

lives in New York, New York
born 1951 in Cullman, Alabama
1975 BA Auburn University,
  Auburn, Alabama
1975-1978 Technische Universität,
  München, West Germany

selected recent exhibitions

1994 *Solo Exhibition,* Oysterponds Historical Society, Orient, New York
1993 *Group Exhibition,* Hampton Square Gallery, Westhampton Beach, New York
1992 *Solo Exhibition,* Soho Photo Gallery, New York, New York
  Solo Exhibition, 2-1/2 x 4-1/2, Fotogalerie, Amsterdam, The Netherlands
  Group Exhibition, The East End Arts Council, Riverhead, New York
  Group Exhibition, Juror, Vicki Goldberg, Maryland Federation of Art,
    Annapolis, Maryland
1991 *Solo Exhibition,* Puchong Gallery, New York, New York
  Solo Exhibition, Dudley Hall Gallery, Auburn University, Auburn, Alabama
  Group Exhibition, Juror, Peter MacGill, Toledo Friends of Photography,
    Toledo, Ohio
  Group Exhibition, The Book Trader Gallery, Philadelphia, Pennsylvania
1990 *Group Exhibition,* City Gallery, New York, New York
  Group Exhibition, Janacek Theatre, Brno, Czechoslovakia
  Group Exhibition, Cork Gallery, Lincoln Center, New York, New York
1989 *Photowork '89,* Juror, Cornell Capa, Poughkeepsie, New York

Man with Elvis Tatoo, 1991, silver gelatin print

Rowland Scherman

lives in Birmingham, Alabama
born 1937 in New York,
New York
1956-1959, Oberlin College,
Oberlin, Ohio

selected recent exhibitions

1991 *Elvis Is Everywhere,* published by Clarkson Potter,
New York, New York

1989 *In View of Home: Alabama Landscape Photographs,*
Huntsville Museum of Art, Huntsville, Alabama (traveled)

1988 *Group Exhibition, Alabama Landscape,* J.R. Leigh Gallery,
Tuscaloosa, Alabama
Solo Exhibition, Birmingham Public Library,
Birmingham, Alabama
Solo Exhibition, Cafe Le Netta, Birmingham, Alabama
Solo Exhibition, Altman-Riddick Museum, Coleman Center,
York, Alabama

1987 *Solo Exhibition,* Alabama State Council on the Arts Gallery,
Montgomery, Alabama

1985 *Solo Exhibition,* Birmingham Frame and Art Gallery,
Birmingham, Alabama
Solo Exhibition, Almost Famous Gallery,
Birmingham, Alabama

1980 *Solo Exhibition (Library Opening),* Birmingham Public
Library, Birmingham, Alabama

1979 *Greater Birmingham Arts Alliance Show,*
Birmingham, Alabama

1976 *Solo Exhibition,* Arno-fini Gallery, Bristol, England
Solo Exhibition, Photographer's Gallery, London, England
Solo Exhibition, Chapter Gallery, Newport, Wales

selected honors, awards, grants

1986 *Media/Photography Grant,* for 50 print essay *"Alabama's
Highway 11,"* Alabama State Council on the Arts,
Montgomery, Alabama

1969 *Photographer of the Year,* Washington, D.C. Art Director's
Association

1968 *Grammy Award,* for *"Bob Dylan Greatest Hits"* (Columbia
Records), National Academy of Recording Arts &
Sciences, Hollywood, California

Alvin C. Sella

lives in Tuscaloosa, Alabama
born 1919 in West Hoboken, New Jersey
Yale University School of Art,
 New Haven, Connecticut
Art Students League, New York, New York
 (studied with Brackman and Bridgeman)
Columbia University, New York, New York
 (studied with Machau)
College of Fine Arts, Syracuse University,
 Syracuse, New York
University of New Mexico, Albuquerque,
 New Mexico
Independent Study in Mexico

selected recent exhibitions

1987 *National Drawing Competition,* Austin Peay University, Clarksville, Tennessee
Group Exhibition, Performing Arts Center, Selma, Alabama
Auburn Works on Paper, Auburn University, Auburn, Alabama

1986 *Alabama Artists Exhibition,* Birmingham Museum of Art, Birmingham, Alabama
Mail Art Show, Birmingham Art Association, Birmingham, Alabama
Alabama University and College Teacher of Painting Exhibition, Visual Arts
 Gallery, University of Alabama at Birmingham, Birmingham, Alabama
Art Faculty Exchange Exhibition, University of Arkansas at Little Rock,
 Little Rock, Arkansas
Group Exhibition, Galleria Atenea, San Miguel de Allende, Guanajuarto, Mexico
48th Annual Exhibition of Contemporary American Painting, Society of the
 Four Arts, Palm Beach, Florida

1985 *Designer Group Show,* Designer Group, Ltd. Baltimore, Maryland (also 1984)
Group Exhibition, Altamont School, Birmingham, Alabama
Birmingham Art Education Council Exhibition, Birmingham Arts Council,
 Birmingham, Alabama
Selma Art Guild, Old Depot Museum, Selma, Alabama
6th Annual Works on Paper and International Invitational Exhibition, Auburn
 University, Auburn, Alabama
Baldwin Community Center Exhibition, Baldwin Community Center,
 Montgomery, Alabama
Alabama Art League, Auburn University, Auburn, Alabama
Department of Art, Faculty Exhibition, Moody Gallery of Art, University of
 Alabama, Tuscaloosa, Alabama (also 1984 and 1983)

1984 *Solo Exhibition,* Galleria Atenea, San Miguel de Allende, Guanajuarto, Mexico

selected honors, awards, grants

1987 *Award, "National Drawing Competition,"* Austin Peay University,
 Clarksville, Tennessee

1986 *Award,* Galleria Atenea, San Miguel de Allenende, Guanajuarto, Mexico

1985 *Award, "Designer Group Show,"* Designer Group, Ltd., Baltimore, Maryland

Apollonian Collapse, 1993, acrylic and oil on canvas with charcoal markings

The Pine Savannah, 1994, prismacolor pencil on paper mounted on board

Steve Shepard

lives in Gautier, Mississippi
born 1955 in Port Arthur, Texas
1976 BFA University of South Alabama,
Mobile, Alabama

selected recent exhibitions

1993 *The Mississippi Artists Collaborative,* Mississippi Museum of Art/
Tupelo, Tupelo, Mississippi

1992 *Solo Exhibition,* Bradley Gallery, Lakeland College, Sheboygan, Wisconsin
The Mississippi Artists Collaborative, Mississippi Museum of Art,
Jackson, Mississippi

1991 *Solo Exhibition,* UMC Gallery, University of Colorado, Boulder, Colorado
The Original Art, Museum of the Society of Illustrators,
New York, New York
Paperworks, '91, Quinlan Art Center, Gainesville, Georgia
The Decorative Impulse, Pennsylvania School of Art and Design,
Lancaster, Pennsylvania
Expressions of Sociometry, Artlink, Fort Wayne, Indiana
Group Exhibition, Delaware Center for Contemporary Art,
Wilmington, Delaware

1990 *Solo Exhibition,* Northeast Missouri State University, Kirksville, Missouri
Solo Exhibition, University of Alabama at Huntsville, Huntsville, Alabama
Solo Exhibition, J.R. Kortman Center for the Arts, Rockford, Illinois
Solo Exhibition, Southeast Massachusetts State, North Dartmouth,
Massachusetts
Nine Mississippi Artists' Show, International Monetary Fund Gallery,
Washington, D.C.
Group Exhibition, The Ohio State University-Mansfield Campus,
Mansfield, Ohio
Group Exhibition, Quincy College, Quincy, Ohio
Group Exhibition, Gasperi Gallery, New Orleans, Louisiana (also 1989)

1988 *Poboye Konate and Steve Shepard,* University of South Alabama,
Mobile, Alabama
Art on Paper, Weatherspoon Art Gallery, University of North Carolina
at Greensboro, Greensboro, North Carolina
*Échange D'Experiences Culturelles entre Le Burkino Faso et Les
Estats-Unis, Poboye Konate et Steve Shepard,* American Cultural Center,
Ouagadougou, Burkino Faso, West Africa
Group Exhibition, 1708 East Main Gallery, Richmond, Virginia
Group Exhibition, Race Street Gallery, Grand Rapids, Michigan
Group Exhibition, Lauren Rogers Museum of Art, Laurel, Mississippi
Contemporary Drawing Invitational, Wake Forest University,
Winston-Salem, North Carolina

selected honors, awards, grants

1993 *Best in Show, "Piccolo Spoleto Fair,"* Charleston, South Carolina
Merit Award, Judge, Dennis R. Barrie, *"Gasparilla Art Festival,"*
Tampa, Florida

1992 *Judges' Choice Award,* Judges, Dennis Adrian and Pat Dandignac,
"Great Gulf Coast Arts Festival," Pensacola, Florida

Charles Smith

lives in Mobile, Alabama
born 1949 in Mobile, Alabama
1973 Bishop State Jr. College, Mobile, Alabama
1975 BS Jackson State University,
    Jackson, Mississippi

selected recent exhibitions

1994 *Solo Exhibition,* Kennedy-Douglass Center for the Arts, Florence, Alabama
1993 *Uncommon Beauty in Common Objects: The Legacy of African American Craft
    Art,* National Afro-American Museum and Cultural Center, Wilberforce, Ohio
    (traveled to American Craft Museum, New York, New York; African American
    Panoramic Experience Museum, Atlanta, Georgia; Museum of African American
    Life and Culture, Dallas, Texas; African American Museum of Fine Arts,
    San Diego, California, and Renwick Gallery, National Museum of American Art,
    Smithsonian Institution, Washington, D.C.)
    African-American Invitational, Alabama State Council on the Arts Gallery,
    Montgomery, Alabama
    Group Exhibition, Fine Arts Museum of the South, Mobile, Alabama
    Southern Clay Invitational, Whiting Art Center, Fairhope, Alabama
1991 *Southern Roots,* Academy of Fine Arts, Birmingham, Alabama (also 1990)
1990 *Solo Exhibition and Workshop,* Alabama A & M University, Huntsville, Alabama
1989 *Solo Exhibition and Workshop,* Louisiana State University,
    Baton Rouge, Louisiana

selected honors, awards, grants

1994 *Individual Artist Fellowship Grant,* Alabama State Council on the Arts,
    Montgomery, Alabama
1993 *First Place, "Eastern Shore Art Association Art Show,"* Whiting Art Center,
    Fairhope, Alabama
1992 *Second Place, "Greater Pensacola Art Festival,"* Pensacola, Florida
1991 *Best of Show, "New Orleans Jazz and Heritage Festival,"* New Orleans, Louisiana
1990 *Award of Distinction, "Art Patrons League/Fine Arts Museum of the South
    Outdoor Arts and Crafts Fair,"* Mobile, Alabama

Untitled, 1987, stoneware

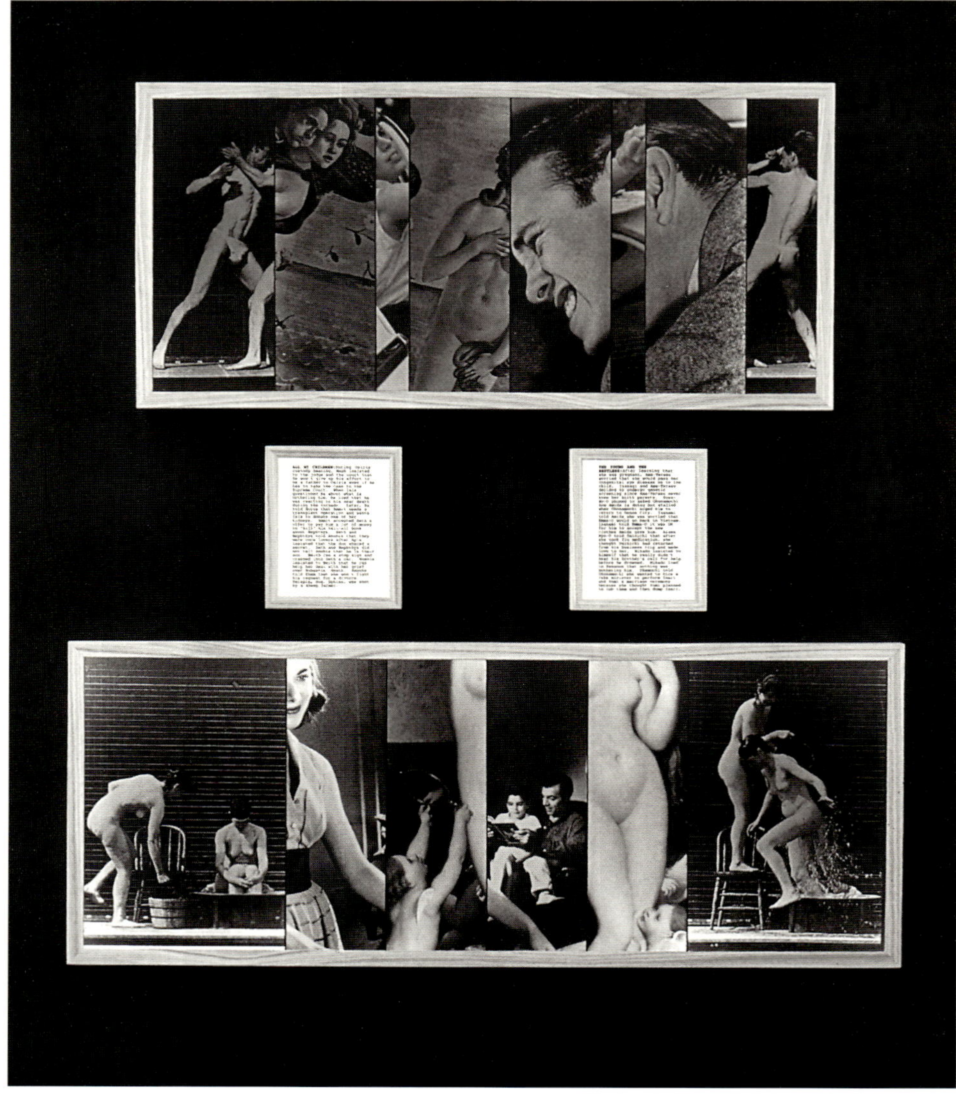

Family Ritual No. 3 & 10, 1994, photomontages mounted on board

Cooper D. Spivey

lives in Birmingham, Alabama
born 1946 in Alexander City, Alabama
1987 BFA University of Alabama,
 Tuscaloosa, Alabama
1991 MA University of Alabama,
 Tuscaloosa, Alabama

selected recent exhibitions

1994 *Solo Exhibition, Family Structures,* Tate Gallery, University of Georgia,
 Athens, Georgia
 Solo Exhibition, Family Structures, Studio 2030, Birmingham, Alabama
 Solo Exhibition, Family Structures, Arts Exchange, Atlanta, Georgia
 Solo Exhibition, Family Structures, Artemesia Gallery, Chicago, Illinois
 Group Exhibition, Domestic Dilemmas (Family Rituals), Space One
 Eleven, Birmingham, Alabama
 Behavior, New Works Gallery, University of Illinois at Chicago,
 Chicago, Illinois

1993 *State of the Art '93,* New England Fine Art Institute, Boston,
 Massachusetts

1992 *Annual Faculty Art Exhibition,* Durbin Gallery, Birmingham-Southern
 College, Birmingham, Alabama
 Art Walk, Studio by the Tracks, Birmingham, Alabama
 Department of Art Faculty Group Exhibition, Visual Arts Gallery,
 University of Alabama at Birmingham, Birmingham, Alabama

1991 *Painters of the 21st Century,* Space One Eleven, Birmingham, Alabama
 Two Decades, Works from the Permanent Collection, Visual Arts Gallery,
 University of Alabama at Birmingham, Birmingham, Alabama

1990 *Group Exhibition,* Space One Eleven, Birmingham, Alabama

1988 *Douglas Baulos and Cooper Spivey,* Space One Eleven,
 Birmingham, Alabama

Melissa Springer

lives in Birmingham, Alabama
born in 1956 in Winston-Salem,
  North Carolina
1974-1976 University of the South,
  Sewanee, Tennesseee
1984 University of Alabama at
  Birmingham, Birmingham, Alabama
1986, 1988, 1989, Maine Photography
  Workshop, Rockport, Maine (studied
  with George Tice, Sally Mann)

selected recent exhibitions

1994 *Solo Exhibition, Michael Tipton, World AIDS Day,* High Museum
  of Art, Atlanta Georgia
Solo Exhibition, Agnes Multimedia Gallery, Birmingham, Alabama
  (also 1993)
Love, Life, Death, Ten Years of Photographic Creation About AIDS,
  FNAC Galeries Photo, Paris, France
Medical Revisions, P.S. 122 Gallery, New York, New York
American Photography, San Antonio Museum of Art,
  San Antonio, Texas
Electric Blanket, Multimedia Slide Show sponsored by Visual AIDS,
  New York, New York

1993 *Solo Exhibition,* Converse College, Spartenburg, South Carolina
Solo Exhibition, National Women's Hall of Fame,
  Seneca Falls, New York
From the Collection of Rena Selfe, Birmingham Museum of Art,
  Birmingham, Alabama

1992 *Solo Exhibition, Julia Tutwiler Women's Prison,* Julia Tutwiler's
  Women's Prison, Wetumpka, Alabama
Encounters 20: Melissa Springer, Huntsville Museum of Art,
  Huntsville, Alabama
Solo Exhibition, Julia Tutwiler's Women's Prison, Gadsden Center
  for the Cultural Arts, Gadsden, Alabama

1991 *Annual Juried Exhibition,* Orlando Museum of Art, Orlando, Florida

1990 *Four Photographers from Alabama,* Armstrong Gallery, Cornell
  College, Mt. Vernon, Iowa
Political Art/Global Concerns, Birmingham Art Association,
  Birmingham, Alabama

1989 *Birmingham Hitachi Exhibition of Contemporary Birmingham
  Artists,* Hitachi Cultural Center, Hitachi, Japan
AIDS, Response of the Artist, Space One Eleven, Birmingham,
  Alabama

selected honors, awards, grants

1994 *Nominated, 1994 Infinity Award in Photojournalism,* International
  Center of Photography, New York, New York
Individual Artist Fellowship Grant, Alabama State Council on the
  Arts, Montgomery, Alabama

Children with AIDS, Alabama, 1992, toned silver gelatin print

Untitled, 1991, monoprint on paper

Scott Stephens

lives in Montevallo, Alabama
born 1954 in Wichita, Kansas
1976 BFA, Washington University,
 St. Louis, Missouri
1976-1977, Graduate Work, The School of the
 Art Institute of Chicago, Chicago, Illlinois
1983 MFA University of Alabama,
 Tuscaloosa, Alabama

selected recent exhibitions

1994 *Recent Works: Scott Stephens,* Maralyn Wilson Gallery, Birmingham, Alabama
 Exhibition of Prints: Scott Stephens, Hammond Hall Gallery, Jacksonville State University,
  Jacksonville, Alabama
 Scott Stephens: Recent Work, Kentuck Museum, Northport, Alabama
 Prints by Gallery Artists, Jan Cicero Gallery, Chicago, Illinois
 University of Alabama Faculty Exhibition, Heritage Hall Museum, Talladega, Alabama
1993 *Scott Stephens: Recent Work,* Shelton State Community College, Tuscaloosa, Alabama
 Selections from the Allrich Gallery: 22nd Anniversary Exhibition, The Allrich Gallery,
  San Francisco, California
 Evans, Jones, Clark, Stephens, One Over One Gallery, Denver, Colorado
 Alabama Print Portfolio, Montgomery Museum of Fine Arts, Montgomery, Alabama
 Selectie Monotypes uit het Frans Masereel Centrum, 1989-1993, Kasterlee, Belgium
 Visual Arts Fellowship Exhibition, Alabama State Council on the Arts Gallery,
  Montgomery, Alabama
 The Door Show, Maralyn Wilson Gallery, Birmingham, Alabama
1992 *Scott Stephens: Recent Work,* Shelton State Community College, Tuscaloosa, Alabama
 Four Printmakers, Jan Cicero Gallery, Chicago, Illinois
 Recent Work: Scott Meyer and Scott Stephens, Bloch Gallery of Art, University of Montevallo,
  Alabama
 David Clark, Jamie Brown, Scott Stephens, One Over One Gallery, Denver, Colorado
 Recent Work: Ted Metz and Scott Stephens, Durbin Gallery, Birmingham-Southern College,
  Birmingham, Alabama
 Prints from the Frans Masereel Center for Printmaking, Zoller Gallery, The Pennsylvania State
  University, University Park, Pennsylvania
1991 *The 5th International Biennial Print Exhibit,* Taipei Fine Arts Museum, Taipei, Taiwan,
  Republic of China
 Metz, Meyers, Stephens, Malone Gallery of Art, Troy State University, Troy, Alabama
1990 *The Red Clay Survey: Second Biennial Exhibition of Contemporary Southern Art,*
  Huntsville Museum of Art, Huntsville, Alabama
 Group Exhibition, Space One Eleven, Birmingham, Alabama
 The Print Show, Maralyn Wilson Gallery, Birmingham, Alabama

selected honors, awards, grants

1993 *Artist-in-Residence,* Cité Internationale des Arts, Paris, France
 Faculty Research Grant, University of Montevallo, Montevallo, Alabama
  (also 1991, 1990, 1988, 1987, and 1985)
1992 *Individual Artist Fellowship,* Alabama State Council on the Arts, Montgomery, Alabama
 Artist-in-Residence, Centrum vor Grafiek Frans Masereel, Kasterlee, Belgium
1987 *Project Grant, The Alabama Print Portfolio,* Alabama State Council on the Arts,
  Montgomery, Alabama
 Distinguished Teacher Award, University of Montevallo, Montevallo, Alabama

Billie Ruth Sudduth

lives in Bakersville, North Carolina
born 1945 in Sewanee, Tennessee
1967 BA Huntingdon College, Montgomery, Alabama
1969 MSW University of Alabama, Tuscaloosa, Alabama

selected recent exhibitions

1994 *The Smithsonian Craft Show,* Smithsonian Institution, Washington, D.C.
1993 *Solo Exhibition,* North Carolina Crafts Gallery, Carrboro, North Carolina
Craft of the Carolinas, Gibbes Museum of Art, Charleston, South Carolina (traveled to Rudolf
E. Lee Gallery, Clemson University, Clemson, South Carolina; Spirit Square for the Arts,
Charlotte, North Carolina; Green Hill Center, Greensboro, North Carolina; Folk Arts Center,
Asheville, North Carolina)
Southeastern Juried Exhibition 1993, Juror, Henry Hopkins, Fine Arts Museum of the South,
Mobile, Alabama
Spotlight '93, Southeast Crafts, Arrowmont School of the Arts and Crafts, Gatlinburg,
Tennessee
Small Expressions, Handweavers Guild of America, James and Meryl Hearst Center for the
Visual Arts, Cedar Falls, Iowa
The Gathering, Bucknell University, Lewisburg, Pennsylvania
Woven, Plaited, Twined, Coiled, Sawtooth Center, Milton Rhodes Gallery, Winston-Salem,
North Carolina
1992 *The Philadelphia Craft Show,* Philadelphia Museum of Art, Philadelphia, Pennsylvania
Wilmington Artists VIII, St. John's Museum of Art, Wilmington, North Carolina (also 1990)
Materials Hard and Soft, Meadows Gallery, Center for the Visual Arts, Denton, Texas
Spotlight '92, American Craft Council, SE Region, Hand Workshop, Richmond, Virginia
Fiber Invitational, Chelsea Gallery, Western Carolina University, Cullowee, North Carolina
1991 *Solo Exhibition,* Fine Arts Center, Francis Marion College, Florence, South Carolina
The Wichita National '91, The Wichita Center for the Arts, Wichita, Kansas
Fiber Celebrated '91, Colorado Springs Fine Arts Center, Colorado Springs, Colorado
34th Chatauqua National Exhibition of American Art, Chautauqua Art Association Galleries,
Chautauqua, New York
Crafts National 25, Zoller Gallery, Pennsylvania State University, University Park, Pennsylvania
A Celebration of Community, Emerging Artist Program-The First Three Years, St. John's
Museum of Art, Wilmington, North Carolina

selected honors, awards, grants

1994 *Visual Arts Fellowship Finalist,* Southern Arts Federation/NEA, Atlanta, Georgia
1993 *Corporate Purchase Award,* "Centerfest," Durham, North Carolina (also 1992)
Corporate Purchase Award, "Springfest," Charlotte, North Carolina (also 1990)
1992 *Award of Honor,* "Boardwalk Art Show," Virginia Beach Center for the Arts, Virginia Beach,
Virginia
Honorable Mention, "Measuring Up 1992," Virginia Beach Center for the Arts, Virginia
Beach, Virginia
1991 *Collector's Award,* "Piedmont Craftsmen," Winston-Salem, North Carolina
1990 *Emerging Artist Grant,* Arts Council of the Lower Cape Fear/North Carolina Arts Council,
Raleigh, North Carolina

Cat's Head Basket, 1994, hand-dyed rattan, natural crushed walnut hull stain,
carved handle with hand hold

Beyond the Dark Leaf, 1993, oil on canvas

John Thomas

lives in Kailua-Kona, Hawaii
born 1927 in Bessemer, Alabama
1951 BA New School for Social Research,
   New York, New York
1946-1948 University of Georgia, Athens, Georgia
1954 MA New York University, New York, New York
1954 Università per Stranieri, Perugia, Italy

selected recent exhibitions

1989 *Visions of the Volcano,* East Hawaii Cutural Center, Hilo, Hawaii (traveled to
   Contemporary Museum in the Honolulu Advertiser Gallery, Honolulu, Hawaii;
   Stones Gallery, Lihue, Kauai, Hawaii; and Hui Noeau Visual Arts Center, Makawao,
   Maui, Hawaii)

1988 *Solo Exhibition, Depictions and Impressions II,* Stones Gallery, Lihue, Kauai, Hawaii
   Solo Exhibition, People of Hawaii, Volcano Art Center, Volcanoes National Park, Hawaii

1987 *Solo Exhibition, Island Mix,* Popoki Gallery, Hilo, Hawaii
   Solo Exhibition, The Hawaii Years 1965-87, The Showcase Gallery, Keauhou-Kona,
   Hawaii

1986 *5th Anniversary Print Exhibition,* The Showcase Gallery, Keauhou-Kona, Hawaii

1985 *Solo Exhibition, Orchids,* The Showcase Gallery, Keauhou-Kona, Hawaii
   Solo Exhibition, Myth, Fire and Foliage, Volcano Art Center, Volcanoes National
   Park, Hawaii
   Solo Exhibition, A Retrospective of Posters and Graphics, Manoa Gallery, Honolulu,
   Hawaii
   Solo Exhibition, Night Images, Gallery EAS, Honolulu, Hawaii

selected honors, awards, grants

1986 *Commendation,* from the Hawaii State House of Representatives, Honolulu, Hawaii

Helen Johnston Vaughn

lives in Huntsville, Alabama
born 1940 in Birmingham,
  Alabama
1960-1963 Howard College,
  Birmingham, Alabama
1964 BA University of Alabama,
  Tuscaloosa, Alabama
1974-1976 Post-Graduate Studies
  University of Alabama at
  Huntsville, Huntsville, Alabama

selected recent exhibitions

1994 *Vivid Color: New Directions in Pastel,* Huntsville Museum of Art,
  Huntsville, Alabama

1993 *Alabama Landscapes,* Wiregrass Museum of Art, Dothan, Alabama
  (traveled)
  Southern Images, Visual Arts Center of Northwest Florida,
  Panama City, Florida
  Biennial Juried Exhibition, Wiregrass Museum of Art,
  Dothan, Alabama
  *The Red Clay Survey: Fourth Biennial Exhibition of
  Contemporary Southern Art,* Huntsville Museum of Art,
  Huntsville, Alabama (also 1990)
  Biennial Juried Exhibition, Wiregrass Museum of Art,
  Dothan, Alabama

1991 *Encounters 16: Helen Vaughn,* Huntsville Museum of Art,
  Huntsville, Alabama

1990 *Art and the Alabama Woman,* Mobile College, Mobile, Alabama
  Opening Exhibition, Gadsden Cultural Arts Foundation,
  Gadsden, Alabama

1989 *Reunion Exhibition,* Wiregrass Museum of Art, Dothan, Alabama
  Alabama Realists Exhibition, New Life Gallery, Montgomery, Alabama

1987 *Exhibition of Hand-Painted Easter Eggs* (Permanent Collection),
  The White House, Washington, D.C.
  Alabama Artists Showcase, Alabama State Council on the Arts Gallery,
  Montgomery, Alabama

1985 *Solo Exhibition,* Market House Museum, Paducah, Kentucky

selected honors, awards, grants

1992 *Merit Award, "The Red Clay Survey: Fourth Biennial Exhibition of
  Contemporary Southern Art,"* Huntsville Museum of Art,
  Huntsville, Alabama

1990 *People's Choice Award, "The Red Clay Survey: Third Biennial Exhibition
  of Contemporary Southern Art,"* Huntsville Museum of Art,
  Huntsville, Alabama

1990 *Award of Distinction* and *Merit Award, "Art and the Alabama Woman, "*
  Mobile College, Mobile, Alabama

1989 *Review Panel Member,* Alabama State Council on the Arts,
  Montgomery, Alabama

A Glass of Lemonade, 1993, pastel on museum board

Eye See Nothing, 1993, day-glow color lithograph

William A. Walmsley

lives in Tallahassee, Florida
born 1923 in Tuscumbia, Alabama
1951 BFA University of Alabama, Tuscaloosa, Alabama
1953 MA University of Alabama, Tuscaloosa, Alabama

selected recent exhibitions

1993 *Ding Dong Daddy: The Lithographs of William Walmsley,* University Gallery, University of North Florida, Jacksonville, Florida

1991 *William A. Walmsley/Ding Dong Daddy,* Virginia Beach Center for the Arts, Virginia Beach, Virginia
Solo Exhibition, University of Tennessee, Chattanooga, Tennessee
Prints from the East, University of Central Arkansas, Conway, Arkansas

1990 *Solo Exhibition,* Polk Community College, Winter Haven, Florida
Solo Exhibition, Professor Emeritus Exhibition, Florida State University, Tallahassee, Florida
American Print Survey/Ding Dong Daddy Oh Me, Morton Museum, University Art Gallery, Baylor University, Waco, Texas
42nd North American Print Exhibition, Boston Printmakers, Fitchburg Art Museum, Fitchburg, Massachusetts
Group Exhibition, Florida State University, Tallahasee, Florida

1989 *Society of American Graphic Artists 63rd National Print Exhibition,* New York, New York
Dakota 100, International Exhibition, University of South Dakota, Vermillion, South Dakota (traveled)
Southern Printmakers '88, Townhouse Gallery, University of South Alabama, Mobile, Alabama

1988 *Group Exhibition,* Kansas State University, Manhattan, Kansas
Prints by Rolling Stone Press, Georgia Institute of Techology, Atlanta, Georgia
40th North American Print Exhibition, Boston Printmakers, Fuller Museum of Art, Brockton, Massachusetts

1987 *63rd Annual International Competition,* The Print Club, Philadelphia, Pennsylvania
National Print and Drawing Exhibition, University of North Dakota, Grand Forks, North Dakota
International Works on Paper, Auburn University, Auburn, Alabama
Group Exhibition, Frans Masareel Center for Printmaking, Kasterlee, Belgium

selected honors, awards, grants

1990 *Museum Committee,* Florida State University Gallery, Tallahassee, Florida (also 1989)
1989 *Alumni Arts Award,* Society of Fine Arts, University of Alabama, Tuscaloosa, Alabama
Museum Committee, Appleton Museum of Art, Ocala, Florida (ongoing)
1986 *Printmaker Emeritus,* Southern Graphics Council
1980 *Juror,* Prints and Drawings Grant Review Committee, National Endowment for the Arts, Washington, D.C.

Jack Whitten

lives in New York, New York
born 1939 in Bessemer, Alabama
1957-1959 Tuskeegee Institute, Tuskeegee, Alabama
1959-1960 Southern University, Baton Rouge,
   Louisiana
1960-1964 The Cooper Union for the Advancement of
   Science and Art, New York, New York

selected recent exhibitions

1994   *Jack Whitten: Recent Paintings,* Horodner Romley Gallery, New York, New York
  Jack Whitten: Paintings from the 70's, Daniel Newburg Gallery, New York, New York
1993   *Reflections of a King,* National Civil Rights Museum, Memphis, Tennessee
  Skin Deep, The New Museum of Contemporary Art, New York, New York
  Faculty Show, Hunter College, New York, New York
  Invitation to a Review, Horodner Romley Gallery, New York, New York
1992   *Solo Exhibition,* Horodner Romley Gallery, New York, New York
  <u>*REVERB*</u> *1960's-1970's,* Horodner Romley Gallery, New York, New York
  Drawing: From Beginning to End, Ben Shahn Galleries, William Paterson College, Wayne,
   New Jersey
  Forms of Abstraction, G.R. N'Namdi Gallery, Columbus, Ohio
  Slow Art, P.S. 1, Long Island City, New York
1991   *Collage: New Application,* Lehman College Art Gallery, Bronx, New York
  The Search for Freedom, African American Abstract Painting 1945-1975, Kenkaleba Gallery,
   New York, New York (traveled)
  Group Exhibition, Reinberger Galleries of the Cleveland Institute of Art, Cleveland, Ohio
  Group Exhibition, College Art Gallery, State University of New York, New Palz, New York
  Expressive Drawings, New York Academy of Art, New York, New York
  *Espiritu & Materia: Estetica Alternativa Norteamericano; Melvin Edwards, Tyrone Mitchell,
   Jack Whitten, William T. Williams,* Museo de Artes Visuales Alejandro Otero, Caracas,
   Venezuela
  Artists Love New York, Marine Midland Branch, New York, New York
  Infusion, Brooklyn College Art Gallery, Brooklyn, New York
  Forms of Abstraction, G.R. N'Namdi Gallery, Birmingham, Michigan
1990   *Jack Whitten,* Newark Museum, Newark, New Jersey
  Jack Whitten: Reconstructions, Cure Gallery, Los Angeles, California
  Reinstallation of Third Floor Galleries, Museum of Modern Art, New York, New York
1989   *Jack Whitten: Urban Abstractions,* G.R.N'Namdi Gallery, Detroit, Michigan
  Introspectives: Contemporary Art by Americans and Brazilians of African Descent,
   The California Afro-American Museum, Los Angeles, California (traveled)
1988   *New York City Works by Twenty One Artists,* One Penn Plaza, New York, New York

selected honors, awards, grants

1984   Sambuca Romana Contemporary Art Fellowship
1976   *Fellowship Recipient,* John Simon Guggenheim Memorial Foundation,
   New York, New York

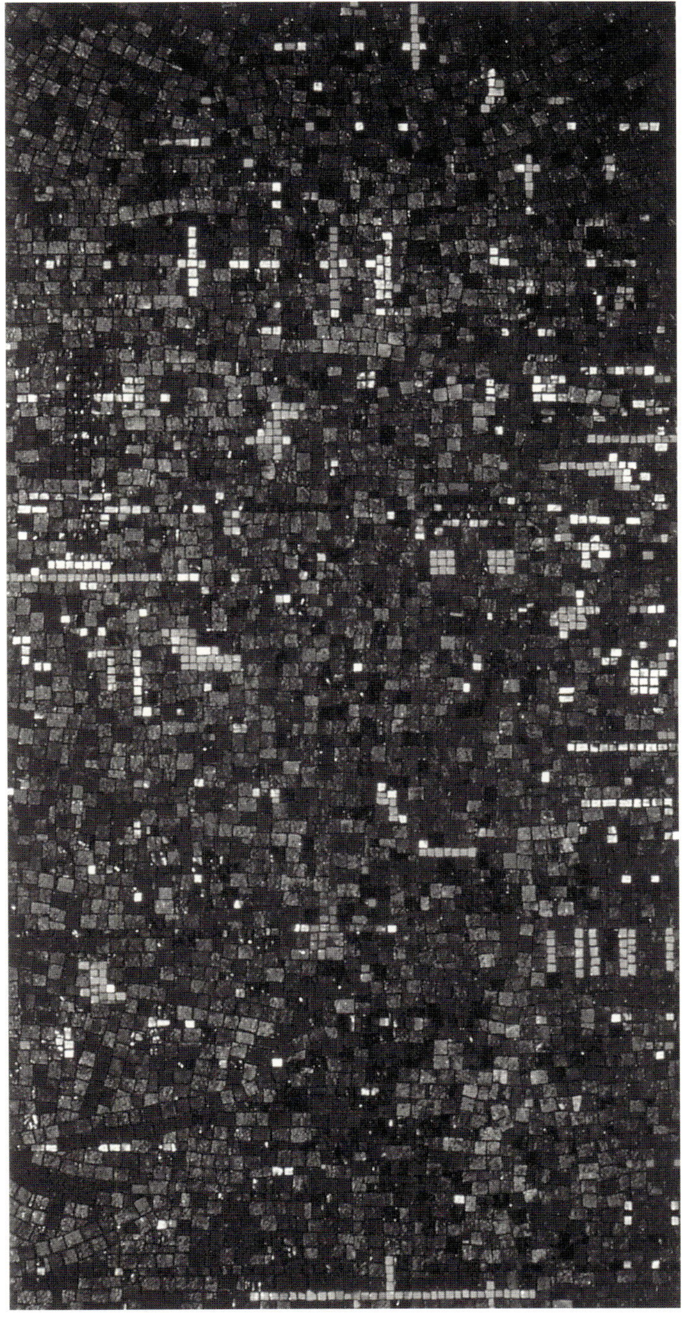

The Cosmic Bopper, 1993, acrylic on canvas

Markets of Kumasi (#4), 1993, mixed media on wood

Hugh O. Williams

lives in Auburn, Alabama
born 1928 in Centre, Alabama
1949 BA Auburn University, Auburn, Alabama
1956 MA Columbia University, New York,
New York

selected recent exhibitions

1994 *Solo Exhibition,* Meridian Museum of Fine Art, Meridian, Mississippi
1993 *Solo Exhibition,* Opelika Art Association Gallery, Opelika, Alabama
1990 *Solo Exhibition,* Whiting Art Center, Fairhope, Alabama
Solo Exhibition, Little House Art Gallery, Birmingham, Alabama
(also 1988 and 1985)
LaGrange National XV, Chattahoochee Valley Art Museum and Lamar Dodd
Art Center, LaGrange College, LaGrange, Georgia
1989 *Birmingham Art Association Biennial V,* The Birmingham Museum of Art ,
Birmingham, Alabama
1985 *Solo Exhibition,* Museum of Arts and Sciences, Macon, Georgia
1983 *Solo Exhibition,* Foundry Gallery, Washington, D.C.

selected honors, awards, grants

1991 *Fulbright-Hays Educational Grant,* West Africa
1987 *A. Atward Kent, Jr. Award,* Society of the Four Arts, Palm Beach, Florida
Reader, Samuel G. Wiener Fund Grant Awards, Atlanta Georgia
1986 *Honorarium Award, "Visual Arts for the Home,"* Atlanta, Georgia
1985 *Alumni Professor Emeritus of Arts,* Auburn University, Auburn, Alabama
1983 *Alumni Professorship of Arts,* Auburn University, Auburn, Alabama
Reviewer, Visual Arts Touring Program, Southern Arts Federation,
Atlanta, Georgia
1980 *Hugh O. Williams Scholarship,* created by the Mississippi Art Colony, Inc.,
Utica, Mississippi

Thornton Willis

lives in New York, New York
born 1936 in Pensacola, Florida
1962 BS University of Southern Mississippi,
Hattiesburg, Mississippi
1966 MFA University of Alabama,
Tuscaloosa, Alabama

selected recent exhibitions

1993 *Solo Exhibition,* Andre Zarre Gallery, New York, New York
1991 *Abstract Painting the 90's,* Curator, Barbara Rose, Andre Emmerich Gallery,
New York, New York
1989 *Dorothy Diener, Peter Voulkis, Thornton Willis,* Twining Gallery, New York,
New York
1988 *Solo Exhibition,* Galerie Nordenhake, Stockholm, Sweden
1987 *Solo Exhibition,* Pensacola Museum of Art, Pensacola, Florida
1986 *Solo Exhibition,* Oscarsson-Siegeltuch, New York, New York
Group Exhibition, Rose Museum, Brandeis University, Waltham,
Massachusetts
Group Exhibition, Cork Gallery, Lincoln Center, New York, New York
Group Exhibition (Inaugural), Oscarsson-Siegeltuch, New York, New York
1985 *Solo Exhibition,* Gloria Luria, Miami, Florida
Solo Exhibition, C.W. Woods Gallery, University of Southern Mississippi,
Hattiesburg, Mississippi
Color Abstraction in the 80's, Bernard M. Baruch College, City University of
New York, New York, New York
Affair of the Heart, Albright-Knox Art Gallery, Buffalo, New York
1984 *Solo Exhibition,* Oscarsson Hood, New York, New York
An International Survey of Recent Painting and Sculpture, Museum of
Modern Art, New York, New York (Re-opening Inaugural)
New Abstraction, Milwaukee Art Museum, Milwaukee, Wisconsin
Ten Years of Contemporary Art, General Electric Corporation (on loan from
the Museum of Modern Art, New York, New York)

selected honors, awards, grants

1991 *Individual Support Grant,* Adolph and Esther Gottlieb Foundation,
New York, New York
1984 *Fellowship in Printmaking,* National Endowment for the Arts,
Washington, D.C.
1980 *Fellowship in Painting,* National Endowment for the Arts, Washington, D.C.
1985 *Outstanding Alumni in the Visual Arts,* University of Southern Mississippi,
75th Anniversary, Hattiesburg, Mississippi
1979 *Fellowship Recipient,* John Solomon Guggenheim Memorial Foundation,
New York, New York

Space Finder, 1992, acrylic on canvas

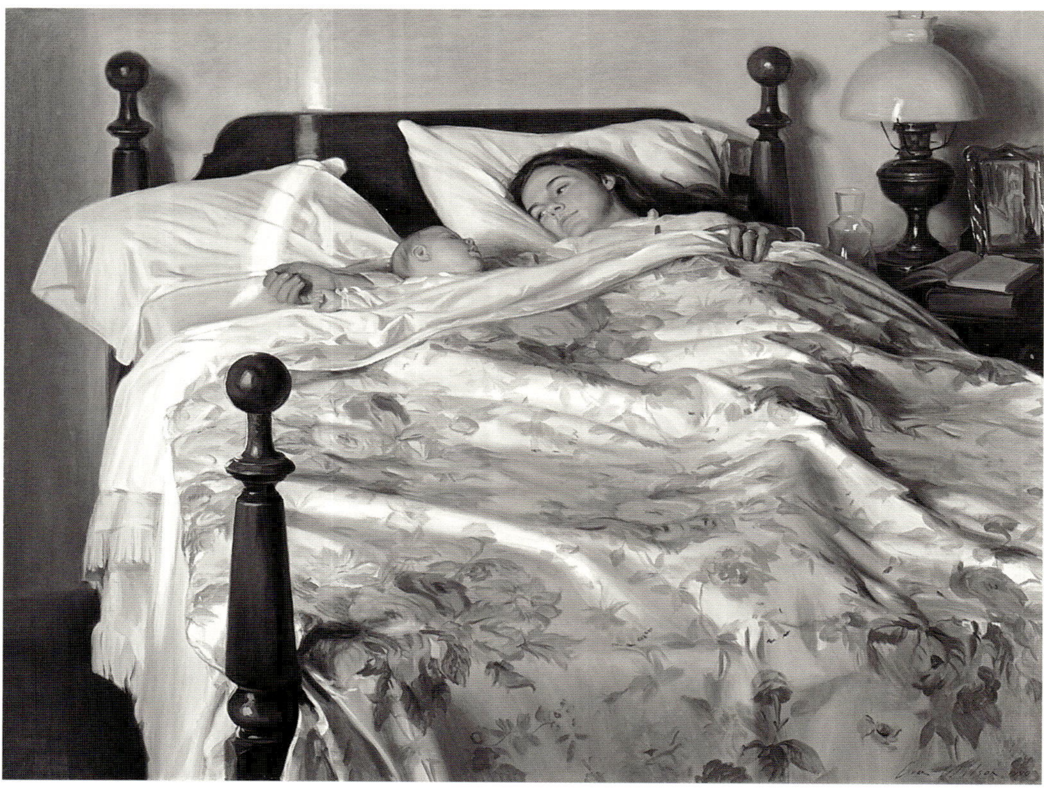

Anita and Elliot, 1989, oil on canvas

Evan C. Wilson

lives in Hoosick, New York
born 1953 in Tuscaloosa, Alabama
1972-1975, Maryland Institute, College
of Art, Baltimore, Maryland (studied
with Joseph Sheppard)
1975-1976 Schuler School of Fine Art,
Baltimore, Maryland

selected recent exhibitions

1994 *Evan Wilson,* Robert M. Hicklin Jr., Inc., Spartanburg, South Carolina
Solo Exhibition, Southern Vermont Art Center, Manchester, Vermont
Evan Wilson, J.R. Leigh Gallery, Tuscaloosa, Alabama (also 1993, 1992,
and 1987-1980)
1993 *Group Exhibition,* John Pence Gallery, San Francisco, California
(also 1992-1988)
1991 *Impressions of America, The Warner Collection of Gulf States Paper
Corporation,* Montgomery Museum of Fine Arts, Montgomery, Alabama
1990 *Solo Exhibition,* John Pence Gallery, San Francisco, California
1989 *Group Exhibition,* J.R. Leigh Gallery, Tuscaloosa, Alabama
(also 1988, 1987 and 1983)
The Food Show, Grand Central Art Galleries, New York, New York
Group Exhibition, Pierre's Gate, Manchester, Vermont
1988 *Mid-Year Show,* Butler Institute of Art, Youngstown, Ohio (also 1973)
Group Exhibition, Stevenson Gallery, Manchester, Vermont
Group Exhibition, Salmagundi Club, New York, New York (also 1987-1984)
1987 *Group Exhibition,* Talisman Gallery, Bartlesville, Oklahoma (also 1986)
1986 *Solo Exhibition,* Bartlesville Community Center Gallery, Bartlesville,
Oklahoma
Group Exhibition, O'Brian's Art Emporium, Scottsdale, Arizona
Portrait Show, Francesca Anderson Gallery, Boston, Massachusetts
Group Show, Knickerbocker Artists, New York, New York (also 1985)
1985 *Gallery Portrait Artists,* Grand Central Art Galleries, New York, New York
Group Exhibition, McKenna Gallery, Charlotte, North Carolina
Group Exhibition, Portraits Inc., New York, New York
Group Exhibition, National Arts Club, New York, New York
(also 1984 and 1983)

selected honors, awards, grants

1987 *Macowin Tuttle Memorial First Prize Award,* Salmagundi Club, New York,
New York
1986 *Salmagundi Club Prize,* Salmugundi Club, New York, New York
Jane Peterson Memorial Award, Salmagundi Club, New York, New York
Gold Medal of Honor, Knickerbocker Club, New York, New York
1985 *Kenneth W. Fitch Award,* Salmagundi Club, New York, New York
Don Donaldson Memorial Award, Salmagundi Club, New York, New York
Alice B. McReynolds Award, Salmagundi Club, New York, New York
Lee M. Loeb Memorial Award, Knickerbocker Artists, New York, New York

Tom Woodward

lives in Opelika, Alabama
born 1949 in Nashville, Tennessee
1967-1968 Auburn University,
Auburn, Alabama

selected recent exhibitions

1994 *Cheaha Exhibition,* Jemison Art Center, Talladega, Alabama
Exhibition South, Tennesse Valley Art Center, Tuscumbia, Alabama
Arts Alive, Kennedy-Douglass Center for the Arts, Florence, Alabama
   (also 1993 and 1992)
1993 *Allied Artists Exhibition,* New York, New York
Art with a Southern Drawl, University of Mobile, Mobile, Alabama
Grand National, Akron, Ohio
Realism 93, Parkersburg Art Center, Parkersburg, West Virginia
Group Exhibition, Montgomery Art Association, Montgomery Museum of
   Fine Arts, Montgomery, Alabama
1992 *Group Exhibition,* New Orleans Art Association, New Orleans, Louisiana
Black and White, Associated Artists of Winston-Salem, Winston-Salem,
   North Carolina
Audubon Artists, New York, New York
Group Exhibition, Harrisburg Art Association, Harrisburg, Pennsylvania
1989 *Solo Exhibition,* Whiting Art Center, Fairhope, Alabama
Group Exhibition, Schwab Festival, Chicago, Illinois (also 1988 and 1987)
1988 *The Subject is Woman,* Partners Gallery, Bethesda, Maryland
Group Exhibition, Spring Hill College, Mobile, Alabama
Call to Rise, Orlando Museum of Art, Orlando, Florida (traveled)
1987 *American Artist Exhibition,* John Pence Gallery, San Francisco, California
   (traveled)
1986 *Solo Exhibition,* Fine Arts Museum of the South, Mobile, Alabama
Mid-America Biennial, Owensboro Museum of Fine Art, Owensboro, Kentucky

selected honors, awards, grants

1994 *Award, "Cheaha Exhibition,"* Jemison Art Center, Talladega, Alabama
Award, "Exhibition South," Tennesssee Valley Art Center, Tuscubmbia, Alabama
Award, "Arts Alive," Kennedy-Douglass Center for the Arts, Florence, Alabama
   (also 1993 and 1992)
1993 *Award, "Art with a Southern Drawl,"* University of Mobile, Mobile, Alabama
1992 *Award, "New Orleans Art Association,"* New Orleans, Louisiana
Award, "Black and White," Associated Artists of Winston-Salem, Winston-Salem,
   North Carolina

Requiem for Winter, 1993, graphite on paper

Temerson, 1971, etching on paper

Richard C. Zoellner

lives in Tuscaloosa, Alabama
born 1908 in Portsmouth, Ohio
1927 Cincinnati Art Academy, Cincinnati, Ohio
1931 Tiffany Foundation, Oyster Bay, New York

selected recent exhibitions

1994 *Birmingham Art Exhibition,* Birmingham Greek Orthodox Cathedral Gala,
Birmingham, Alabama

1993 *Group Exhibition Mayab, Eight Points of View,* Alabama Museum of Natural History,
The University of Alabama, Tuscaloosa, Alabama

1992 *Solo Exhibition, Impressions of Yucatan,* Alabama Museum of Natural History,
The University of Alabama, Tuscaloosa, Alabama

1989 *Richard Zoellner,* Jacksonville State University, Jacksonville, Alabama

1984 *Solo Exhibition, Artist-in-Residence,* Albany State College, Albany, Georgia

1981 *Richard Zoellner: Print Retrospective,* Huntsville Museum of Art, Huntsville, Alabama

1979 *Richard Zoellner: Paintings, Prints and Drawings 1970/1979,* Garland Hall Art Gallery,
The University of Alabama, Tuscaloosa, Alabama

selected honors, awards, grants

1985 *Distinguished Artist Award,* The University of Alabama Society of Fine Arts,
Tuscaloosa, Alabama

1980 *Purchase Award,* National Print Exhibition, Silvermine Gallery, New Canaan, Connecticut

1979 *Printmaker Emeritus,* Southern Graphics Council, Annual Regional Meeting, University of
Mississippi, Oxford, Mississippi

The Exhibition Checklist

Height precedes width and depth; all dimensions are in inches.
• Indicates works illustrated.

Jere H. Allen

• *Fathers and Sons,* 1994
oil on linen
72 x 66
courtesy the artist

Reflections, 1994
oil on linen
42 x 36
courtesy the artist

Paula Barr

• *Taliesen Valley,* 1991
cibachrome print laminated
    to plexiglas
40 x 120
courtesy the artist

Gas Lit Mardi Gras, 1994
iris print on watercolor paper
31 3/4 x 44 1/4
courtesy the artist

Grotto, 1994
iris print on watercolor paper
31 3/4 x 44 1/4
courtesy of the artist

Raine Bedsole

• *Spirit House—Lotus,* 1991
mixed media on wood
29 x 23
courtesy the artist

Spirit House—Torso, 1991
mixed media on wood
29 x 23
courtesy the artist

Roger Brown

• *Americana/Benton, O'Keefe, Rivera
    & Hartley,* 1988
oil on canvas
83 x 96
courtesy Phyllis Kind Gallery, Chicago,
    Illinois & New York, New York

Burners, Burglars/Beaters, 1992
oil on canvas
48 x 72
courtesy Phyllis Kind Gallery, Chicago,
    Illinois & New York, New York

Rosa Californica, 1994
oil on canvas
72 x 48
courtesy Phyllis Kind Gallery, Chicago,
    Illinois & New York, New York

Richmond Burton

Flesh Fusion, 1993
oil on linen
24 x 30
courtesy the artist

• *Of His Bones are Coral Made,* 1993
oil on linen
78 x 99
courtesy the artist and Matthew
    Marks Gallery, New York, New York

Untitled, 1993
oil on linen
32 x 40
courtesy the artist

Scott Burton

• *Semi-Circle Table,* designed 1988
    with fabrication 1989
(edition of 5, 3 prototypes)
mild steel
28 1/4 x 54 1/2 x 22
courtesy the Estate of Scott Burton
    and Max Protetch Gallery, New York,
    New York

Oak Chair, 1989
(edition of 12, 1 prototype)
stained oak
40 x 21 1/4 x 22 1/2
courtesy the Estate of Scott Burton
    and Max Protetch Gallery, New York,
    New York

Gerald Lee Cannon

• *Cul-De-Sac,* 1990
ink & enamel on wood
25 1/2 x 80
courtesy the artist

Members (EGBDF), 1990
wood, glass, HCP prints
60 x 144
courtesy the artist

Paula Chamlee

Pojoaque, New Mexico, 1991
silver chloride contact print
8 x 10
courtesy the artist

• *Prague, Czech Republic,* 1994
silver chloride contact print
8 x 10
courtesy the artist

Gary Chapman

• *Magnetic Hysteresis,* 1992
oil on linen
137 x 137
courtesy the artist

Ein Anderes Grabmal, 1993
charcoal & conte crayon on paper,
    over oil on canvas
36 x 89
courtesy the artist

William Christenberry

*Kudzu Creeping Across Road,
    Near Moundville, Alabama,* 1983
EK 74 photograph
image: 17 1/2 x 22
sheet: 20 x 24
courtesy the artist & Pace/MacGill
    Gallery, New York, New York

*Landscape and Silo, Near Tuscaloosa,
    Alabama,* 1990
EK 74 photograph
image: 17 1/2 x 22
sheet: 20 x 24
courtesy the artist & Pace/MacGill
    Gallery, New York, New York

Clan Dolls, 1992
mixed media
four, 17 x 7 (each)
courtesy the artist & Pace/MacGill
    Gallery, New York, New York

• *Clan Dolls,* 1992
EK 74 photograph
image: 9 x 6
sheet: 17 x 7 (each of three)
courtesy the artist & Pace/MacGill
    Gallery, New York, New York

Chip Cooper

Dawn Light On Interior, Dicksonia,
1993
cibachrome print
30 x 24
collection of CKM Press, Tuscaloosa,
Alabama
from the collection of *Silent in the Land*

• ***Stairwell, Barton Hall (ca. 1847),*** 1993
cibachrome print
24 x 30
collection of CKM Press, Tuscaloosa,
Alabama
from the collection of *Silent in the Land*

Suzan Courtney

Tuscumbia, 1992 - 1993
oil on canvas
38 x 42
courtesy the artist

• ***Andalusia,*** 1993
oil on canas
38 x 50
courtesy the artist

Casey Downing, Jr.

Circular XXV, 1993
fabricated bronze
74 x 33 x13
courtesy the artist

• ***Circular XXXV,*** 1994
fabricated bronze
13 x 15 x 4
courtesy the artist

Alice Hohenberg Federico

Heart Afire, 1994
glazed white earthenware
2 1/2 x 12 1/2
courtesy the artist & Monty Stabler
Galleries, Birmingham, Alabama

Winged Heart, 1994
glazed white earthenware
3 x 12 1/2
courtesy the artist & Monty Stabler
Galleries, Birmingham, Alabama

• ***Wounded Heart,*** 1994
glazed white earthenware
3 x 13
courtesy the artist & Monty Stabler
Galleries, Birmingham, Alabama

Frank Fleming

• ***Parrot Chair,*** 1980
cast bronze
24 x 12 x 9 5/8
Collection of the Birmingham Museum
of Art; Museum purchase with
matching funds provided by friends
of the artist, Rich's and the National
Endowment for the Arts, a federal
agency

Container, 1992
porcelain
25 x 48 x 11
courtesy the artist

Maud Gatewood

• ***Snow and Wind,*** 1977
acrylic on canvas
60 x 72 1/4
courtesy Somerhill Gallery, Chapel Hill,
North Carolina

Searching for Heroes, 1989
arcylic on canvas
60 x 72
courtesy Somerhill Gallery, Chapel Hill,
North Carolina

Joseph W. Gluhman

Beach, 1993
cibachrome II print
11 x 14
courtesy the artist

Storm, 1993
cibachrome II print
11 x 14
courtesy the artist

• ***Burning Landscape,*** 1994
cibachrome II print
11 x 14
courtesy the artist

Guy Goodwin

• ***Membrane,*** 1991
oil on linen
72 x 98
courtesy the artist

Untitled, 1993
watercolor, gouache, magic marker
17 1/2 x 24 1/2
courtesy the artist

Gerald Hayes

Green Beret, 1987
acrylic on canvas
48 x 60
courtesy the artist

• ***Solar Cuts,*** 1988
acrylic on wood
29 x 28
courtesy the artist

Wright House, 1993
acrylic on wood
22 x 32
courtesy the artist

Cham Hendon

The Club II, 1992
acrylic on canvas
24 x 22
courtesy the artist & Monty Stabler
Galleries, Birmingham, Alabama

Tom's Room, 1992
acrylic on canvas
18 x 22
courtesy the artist & Monty Stabler
Galleries, Birmingham, Alabama

• ***Bessy,*** 1994
acrylic on canvas
42 x 44
courtesy the artist & Monty Stabler
Galleries, Birmingham, Alabama

Edward Lee Hendricks

• ***1990-II,*** 1990
stainless steel, aluminum, painted
brass, gold leaf, level
64 x 18 x 8
courtesy the artist

1995-I, 1995
aluminum, lacquer, gold leaf
62 diam. x 2
courtesy the artist

Chester Higgins, Jr.

*My Great-Aunt Shugg Lampley-New
   Brockton,* 1968
silver gelatin print
20 x24
courtesy the artist

*Any Father Praying over Any
   Son-Ghana,* 1973
silver gelatin print
20 x 24
courtesy the artist

Islamic Face-New York, 1990
silver gelatin print
20 x 24
courtesy the artist

• *Pole Man on River Niger-Mali,* 1993
silver gelatin print
20 x 24
courtesy the artist

Jackson Hill

• *Life of the Soul,* 1994
iris print on watercolor paper
11 x 14
courtesy the artist

Bienville Tunnel, 1994
iris print on watercolor paper
11 x 11
courtesy the artist

Nall Hollis (Nall)

Untitled, 1977
graphite on paper
75 x 19 1/2
collection of Arthur Roger

• *Portrait of Sheree,* 1990-1994
mixed media
26 x 25
collection of Dr. and Mrs. Gilbert
   M. Aust

Mike Howard

• *Bill & Neils, Phenix City,* 1993
acrylic & varnish on canvas
72 x 96
courtesy the artist

Central Stadium, Phenix City, 1993
acrylic & varnish on canvas
72 x 96
courtesy the artist

Steven Bernard Jones

Slave to a Nation, 1990
mixed media
36 x 10 x 10
collection of Jane Schweppe

• *Holy Annihilation,* 1993
mixed media
30 x 18 x 12
courtesy the artist

Dale Kennington

• *Contemporary Frieze,* 1994
oil on canvas
42 x 84
courtesy the artist

Neighborhood Bar, 1994
oil on canvas
40 x 50
courtesy the artist

Janice Kluge

• *Then She Was Gone,* 1991
wood, metal, & sandblasted glass
26 x 24 x 15
courtesy Connell Gallery,
   Atlanta, Georgia

The Voyage, 1991
fabricated brass, cast bronze & glass
84 x 12 x 14
courtesy Connell Gallery,
   Atlanta, Georgia

Cam Langley

• *Red Bouquet,* 1985
blown glass
21 x 13 x 7
courtesy the artist

Pink Bouquet, 1987
blown glass
22 x 12 x 6
courtesy the artist

Frances de La Rosa

Biographical Landscape #7, 92.17,
   1992
oil on canvas
73 x 59 1/2
courtesy Phyllis Weil Gallery,
   New York, New York

• *Biographical Landscape #10, 92.18,*
   1992
oil on canvas
65 1/2 x 46 3/4
courtesy Phyllis Weil Gallery,
   New York, New York

Virginia Levie

Foot, 1993
mixed media on paper
12 x 12
courtesy the artist

• *Sarge,* 1993
mixed media on canvas
38 x 50
courtesy the artist

Untitled (Hand Series), 1995
mixed media on paper
10 x 11
courtesy the artist

Rick Lowe

• *Untitled-Triptych,* 1994
mixed media
46 x 18 x 6 1/2 (each)
courtesy the artist

Tierney LaRon Malone

Store Cans, 1993
mixed media
36 x 42
courtesy the artist

• *The Temple of the Familiar,* 1994
mixed media
72 x 24 x 48
courtesy the artist

Ed McGowin

• *Metropolitan Adults,* 1991
oil on canvas with painted wood frame
52 x 52
courtesy the artist

Big Daddy, 1992
polychrome patinated bronze
13 1/2 x 8 1/4 x 8 1/2
courtesy the artist

Big Mama, 1992
polychrome patinated bronze
13 x 7 x 8 1/2
courtesy the artist

Big Daddy (Closed), 1992
dry pigment & graphite on paper
30 x 23
courtesy the artist

Big Daddy (Opened), 1992
dry pigment & graphite on paper
30 x 23
courtesy the artist

Big Mama (Closed), 1992
dry pigment & graphite on paper
30 x 23
courtesy the artist

Big Mama (Opened), 1992
dry pigment & graphite on paper
30 x 23
courtesy the artist

Ted Metz

• *Faultzone*, 1986
aluminum, slate & painted steel
10 x 24 x 20 1/4
courtesy the artist

Suspect Terrain, 1987
painted steel
8 x 25 x 22
courtesy the artist

Lanford Monroe

Algonquin Reflections, 1989
oil on board
23 x 36
courtesy the artist

• *Sunday Morning*, 1990
oil on panel
35 x 50
collection of the Huntsville Museum of
Art, Huntsville, Alabama

Deborah Muirhead

*Elegy Suite #1, #3, #4, #5, #6, •#7,
#9, #11*, 1994
oil, graphite & tempera on paper
15 x 11 (each)
courtesy the artist

Pat Mulherin

Untitled, 1992
silver print
11 x 14
courtesy the artist

• *Live Oaks*, 1994
silver print
20 x 24
courtesy the artist

Janet Nolan

Sparrow's Nest # 7, 1988
pastel on paper
22 x 30
collection of John E. Daniel

• *Web*, 1994
metal of discarded umbrellas &
broken glass
144 x 122 x 48
courtesy the artist

Matt Nolen

Taste Trophy, 1994
glazed porcelain and earthenware
17 1/2 x 15 1/2 x 8
courtesy Garth Clark Gallery,
New York, New York & Los Angeles,
California

• *Wedding Urn*, 1994
glazed porcelain
22 x 10 x 7
courtesy Garth Clark Gallery,
New York, New York &
Los Angeles, California

Craig Nutt

• *Celery Chair with Peppers, Carrots
& Snow Pea*, 1993
swiss pear and leather
37 x 19 x 22
courtesy Connell Gallery,
Atlanta, Georgia

Radish Salad Bowl, 1993
cherry and maple
57 x 22 x 22
collection of Lewis F. Fitts

David Parrish

Déjà Vu: Double Bogey Popup, 1994
oil on canvas
57 x 67
courtesy Louis K. Meisel Gallery,
New York, New York

Wonder Woman, 1993
oil on canvas
67 x 100 1/2
courtesy Louis K. Meisel Gallery,
New York, New York

Dennis Potter

• *Ring Round Rosie*, 1993
oil on canvas
54 x 26
courtesy the artist & Stephen Wirtz
Gallery, San Francisco, California

Untitled, 1993
monotype on paper
12 x 12
courtesy the artist & Stephen Wirtz
Gallery, San Francisco, California

Ring with Ghosts, 1994
oil on canvas
44 x 44
courtesy the artist & Steven Wirtz
Gallery, San Francisco, California

Stephen Rolfe Powell

(assisted by Che Rhodes, Brook White,
& Paul Nelson)
• *Addiction Cleavage Johnson*, 1993
blown glass
32 x 21 x 11
collection of Dr. & Mrs. Robert
Cumming

Bodacious Gasp Johnson, 1994
blown glass
30 x 24 x 6
courtesy the artist

Joe Price

• *Egg Series VI: Knife*, 1988
screen serigraph on paper
9 x 12
courtesy the artist

Pomegranates, 1989
screen serigraph on paper
10 1/2 x 13
courtesy the artist

Jim Richard

Facing the Sculpture, 1989
acrylic on canvas
18 3/4 x 19 3/4
courtesy Arthur Roger Gallery,
 New Orleans, Louisiana

Facing the Sculpture IV, 1990
acrylic on canvas
21 x 27
courtesy Arthur Roger Gallery,
 New Orleans, Louisiana

• *Owning Modern Sculpture,* 1993
mixed media on paper
30 x 22 1/2
courtesy Arthur Roger Gallery,
 New Orleans, Louisiana

Owning Modern Sculpture, 1993
mixed media on paper
30 x 22 1/2
courtesy Arthur Roger Gallery,
 New Orleans, Louisiana

Sonja Rieger

• *Night Puddle,* 1989
cibachrome
16 x 20
courtesy the artist

Bell System Manhole Cover, 1992
cibachrome
16 x 20
courtesy the artist

Mary Ann Sampson

• *An Opera in My Barn,* 1994
mixed media
36 x 36 x 20
courtesy the artist

It's in the Bag, 1994
mixed media
36 x 36 x 20
courtesy the artist

David Sandlin

• *Satin Sheets (Struggle for 1st
 Spouses' Soul in a Motel Room),*
 1990
oil on canvas
72 x 140
courtesy the artist

Waltz Across Sinland, 1991
oil on canvas
60 x 96
courtesy the artist

Robert A. Schaefer, Jr.

Kate and Megan, 1986
silver gelatin print
16 x 20
collection of Philip Morris Corporation

Sonnya As Josephine Baker, 1990
silver gelatin print
16 x 20
courtesy the artist

• *Rainer,* 1991
silver gelatin print
16 x 20
collection of Rainer Fetting

Rowland Scherman

Lobby, Graceland, 1991
silver gelatin print
11 x 14
courtesy the artist

• *Man with Elvis Tatoo,* 1991
silver gelatin print
11 x 14
courtesy the artist

Store Window, Memphis, 1991
silver gelatin print
11 x 14
courtesy the artist

Alvin C. Sella

• *Apollonian Collapse,* 1993
acrylic and oil on canvas with charcoal
 markings
64 x 76
courtesy the artist

Space Movement, 1994
oil on canvas
60 x 65
collection of Roger Meadows

Steve Shepard

The Bayou, 1994
prismacolor pencil on paper mounted
 on board
72 x 120
courtesy the artist

• *The Pine Savannah,* 1994
prismacolor pencil on paper mounted
 on board
72 x 102
courtesy the artist

Charles Smith

Ceremonial Face Jug, 1980
glazed stoneware
15 x 8 1/2 x 8 1/2
courtesy the artist

• *Untitled,* 1987
stoneware
16 x 9 1/2 x 91/2
 courtesy the artist

Designed Tripod Jar, 1989
11 x 9 1/2 x 9 1/2
stoneware
courtesy the artist

Cooper D. Spivey

• *Family Ritual No. 3,* 1994
photomontage mounted on board
62 x 50 x 2
courtesy the artist

• *Family Ritual No. 10,* 1994
photomontage mounted on board
42 x 20 x 2
courtesy the artist

Melissa Springer

Children with AIDS, Alabama, 1993
toned silver gelatin print
16 x 20
courtesy the artist

• *Children with AIDS, Alabama,* 1992
toned silver gelatin print
16 x 20
courtesy the artist

Children with AIDS, Alabama, 1992
toned silver gelatin print
16 x 20
courtesy the artist

Scott Stephens

• *Untitled,* 1991
monoprint on paper
42 x 34
courtesy the artist

Untitled, 1993
monoprint on paper
34 x 42
courtesy the artist

Billie Ruth Sudduth

A Matter of Perspective, 1994
hand-dyed rattan, vine rattan,
  seagrass & coir
15 x 8 x 8
courtesy the artist

• *Cat's Head Basket*, 1994
hand-dyed rattan, natural crushed
  walnut hull stain, carved handle
  with hand hold
19 x 18 x 18
courtesy the artist

John Thomas

Boy with Goldfish # 1 (Rainbow Birth),
  1977
oil on canvas
60 x 50
collection of Mrs. Cornelia Lazenby

In Pele's Path, 1991
oil on canvas
48 x 32
courtesy the artist

• *Beyond the Dark Leaf*, 1993
oil on canvas
48 x 52
courtesy the artist

Helen Johnston Vaughn

• *A Glass of Lemonade*, 1993
pastel on museum board
30 x 40
collection of Dr. & Mrs. Paul McDowell

Meeting Herself Coming and Going, 1994
charcoal & pastel pencil on
  watercolor paper
36 x 41
collection of Sis Wallace Lester

William A. Walmsley

• *Eye See Nothing*, 1993
day-glow color lithograph
22 x 28
courtesy the artist

Eye See Nothing, 1993
day-glow colored lithograph
22 x 28
courtesy the artist

Jack Whitten

• *The Cosmic Bopper*, 1993
acrylic on canvas
96 x 48
courtesy Horodner Romley Gallery,
  New York, New York

The Russian Bird, 1993
acrylic on canvas
96 x 48
courtesy Horodner Romley Gallery,
  New York, New York

Hugh O. Williams

Markets of Kumasi (#3), 1993
mixed media on wood
96 x 48
collection of E. Dulton

• *Markets of Kumasi (#4)*, 1993
mixed media on wood
96 x 48
courtesy the artist

Thornton Willis

Montecello, 1991
acrylic on canvas
46 1/2 x 35
courtesy the artist

• *Space Finder*, 1992
acrylic on canvas
41 x 35 5/8
courtesy the artist

Evan C. Wilson

• *Anita and Elliot*, 1989
oil on canvas
40 x 52
courtesy the artist

Nude with Chinese Robe, 1993
oil on canvas
40 x 50
collection of Dr. & Mrs. Walter Bishop

Tom Woodward

3rd Room, Oceanside, 1983
graphite on paper
9 1/2 x 17 3/8
Collection of the Mobile Museum of Art,
  Purchased with the proceeds from
  The Outdoor Arts & Crafts Fair
  cosponsored by the Art Patrons
  League and the Mobile Museum of Art

• *Requiem for Winter*, 1993
graphite on paper
29 x 27
courtesy the artist

Richard C. Zoellner

• *Temerson*, 1971
etching on paper
29 x 19 3/4
courtesy the artist

Arrangement, 1978
etching on paper
24 x 18
courtesy the artist

Design & Illustration:
Altherr Howard Design

Photography Credits:
Birmingham Museum of Art, Alabama
Chester Higgins, Jr.,
   Copyrighted, All Rights Reserved
Bob Gathany, Huntsville, Alabama
Bill Jacobson, New York
Phyllis Kind Gallery, Chicago & New York
Malama Arts, Inc., Honolulu
Louis K. Meisel Gallery, New York
Ric Moore Photographs, Fairhope, Alabama
Arthur Roger Gallery, New Orleans
Max Protech Gallery, New York
Weatherspoon Art Gallery, University of
   North Carolina at Greensboro
The Individual Artists

Printing:
Golden Rule Printing

Separations & Film:
O'Neals

*The production of this catalogue has
been made possible by a grant from the
Alabama State Council on the Arts,
Montgomery, Alabama.*